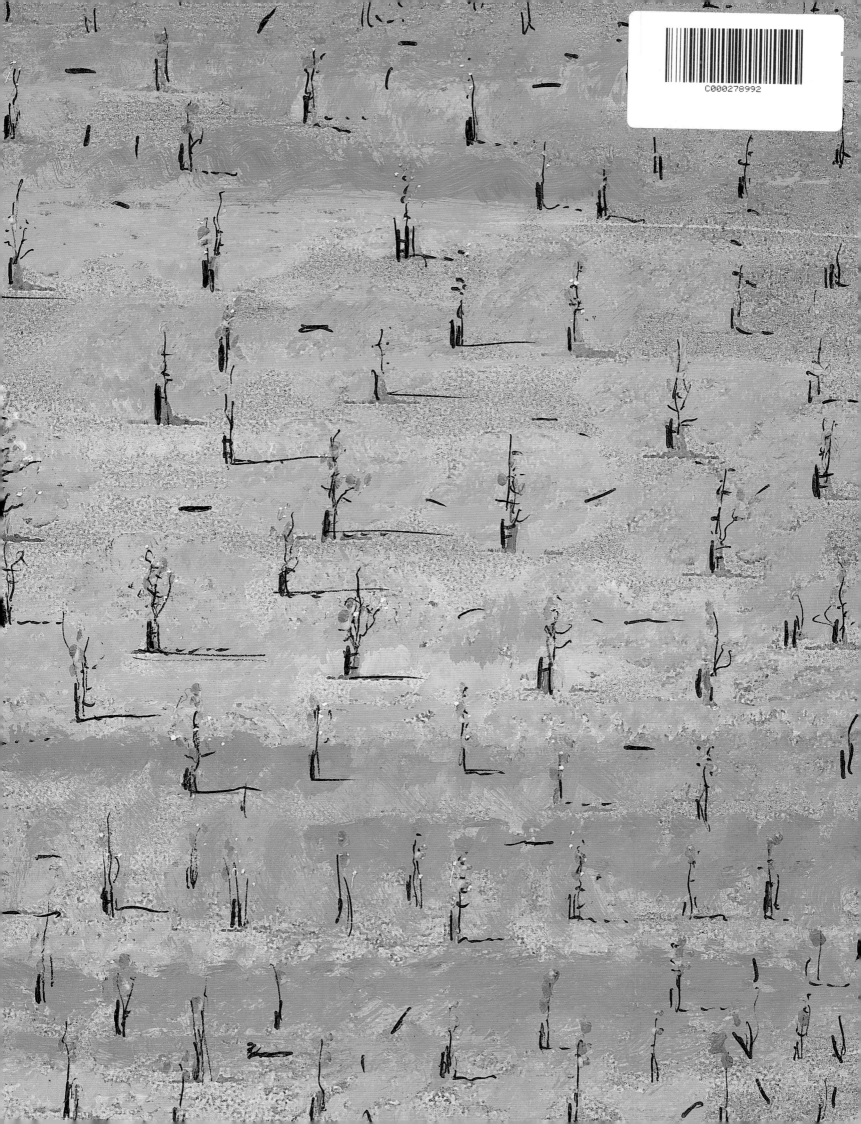

THE GLORIOUS TREES OF GREAT BRITAIN

PIERS BROWNE

THE GLORIOUS TREES OF GREAT BRITAIN

FOREWORD BY H.R.H. PRINCE CHARLES

INTRODUCTIONS BY DAVID BELLAMY

JOHN MURRAY

IN ASSOCIATION WITH THE SHORTHORN PRESS

First published in Great Britain 2002
by The Shorthorn Press
and distributed by John Murray (Publishers) Ltd
50 Albemarle Street, London W1S 4BD

Foreword copyright © HRH The Prince of Wales 2002
Art copyright © Piers Browne 2002
Introductions to species copyright © David Bellamy 2002
Poetry and Prose copyright © The contributors (see Acknowledgements)

ISBN 0 7195 60357

British Library Cataloguing-in-Publication data
A catalogue record for this book is available from the British Library

Designed by Phil Abel at Hand & Eye Letterpress
Printed in Great Britain by York City Printers

I have etched the trees I liked but had to leave out so many others which I both liked, knew of and was told about. However what is left is in memory of our lost elms and dedicated to the noble ambition of the Conservation Foundation and others to replant them in Britain.

This book is also dedicated to a lover of Fine Art and patron of Piers, Massimo Brooke.

It is dedicated too to those farmers who recently lost all their stock in the recent abominable foot and mouth epidemic. These lines by Charlotte Mew from her poem *May, 1915*, sympathise in one with both blood spilt and nature destroyed, then rejuvenated:

Let us remember, Spring will come again
To the scorched, blackened woods, where the wounded trees
Wait, with their old wise patience for the heavenly rain,
Sure of the sky: sure of the sea to send its healing breeze,
Sure of the sun. And even to these
Surely the Spring, when God shall please,
Will come again like a divine surprise
To those who sit today with their great Dead, hand in their hands,
Eyes in their eyes,
At one with love, at one with Grief: blind to the scattered things and changing skies.

The Challenge: Elms Long Gone

CONTENTS

ACKNOWLEDGEMENTS

Firstly, the author and publisher are grateful to his Royal Highness Prince Charles for the foreword and David Bellamy for his tree introductions; also to David Shreeve, with David Bellamy a director of The Conservation Society in London, whose help, with their PR, Lynne Frankland, has been invaluable; Nigel Forde, Antony Dunn and Margaret Whyte for composing such perfect poems for the book; Lorna Dales for organising and assisting with the extra tedious and long job of collating and annotating the poems, prose, pictures and even acknowledgements: thanks to my children Christopher and Kate for the preliminary photographs of the etchings, Neil St Quinton for taking the actual photographs for the book and Andrew Kinnear, Stephen Collier and the director, George Shelley of York City Printers, for their great help in printing the book. Thank you Peter Carpenter and the Hall family of John Tainton Steel Stockholders of Kidderminster for their generous donation of superb steel so faithful in the printing of colours off etched surfaces. Thanks to Phil Abel of Hand & Eye Letterpress for exquisite typographic design and to John Murray for accepting the tome into their catalogue.

Thank you for the printing of poems to John Ashberry *Some Trees* published by Carcanet Press; Clifford Bax *Hot Silence*, reproduced by kind permission of PFD on behalf of the Estate of Clifford Bax; John Murray Ltd for permission to quote John Betjeman; some lines on maples by L. F. J. Brimble from *Trees of Britain* published by Macmillan; John Burnside for *Something is in the Wood* extracted from *Common Knowledge* published by Secker & Warburg used with permission of The Random House Group Limited; Lavinia Greenlaw *Landscape* from *From a World Where News Travelled Slowly* published by Faber & Faber; Seamus Heaney *Song* from *Field Work*, published by Faber & Faber and for two verses from *Sweeney's Flight*; Elaine Feinstein herself for permission to print *The Magic Apple Tree* from *Sundance in Sawston* published with permission to reproduce by Hutchinson; John Hegley *Dog* by kind permission of Methuen Publishing Limited; the late Laurie Lee for the extract from *Cider with Rosie* published by Hogarth Press used by permission of the Random House Group Limited; Dr Alistair Lewis for his learned prose on the eucalyptus; Michael Longley *The Beech Tree* from *The Weather in Japan* published by Jonathan Cape used by permission of The Random House Group Limited; Norman Maccaig for extracts from *Firewood* and *Spring Day* from *Collected Poems* published by The Hogarth Press and used by permission of the Random House Group; Louis Macniece for extracts from *Tree Party* from *Collected Poems* published by Faber & Faber used by permission of David Higham Associates Limited; John Masefield *Twilight* by permission of The Society of Authors as the Literary Representatives of the Estate of John Masefield; H. V. Morton *In Search of Scotland* used by kind permission of Methuen Publishing Limited; Alice Oswald for *A Wood coming into Leaf* from *The Thing in the Gap Stone Stile* published by The Oxford University Press; Thomas Pakenham for some lines from *Meetings with Remarkable Trees* used by kind permission of Cassell & Co; Kathleen Raine from *Childhood: The Lost Country* (1971) by kind permission of Golgonooza Press; Nicholas Rhea for writing such learned notes for the book on the Fortingall Yew; Robin Robertson *Hill-Fort* from *A Painted Field* published by permission of Picador; Siegfried Sassoon *October Trees* by kind permission of George Sassoon; Carole Satyamurti *This Morning* from *Selected Poems* published by Bloodaxe Books; Vernon Scannell *Poet Tree* by kind permission of the author; Dylan Thomas *In my Craft or Sullen Art* and an extract from *Fern Hill* from *Collected Poems* published by J. M. Dent used by permission of David Higham Associates Limited.

Finally, thank you to Juanita DeSilva of Paul Simon Music and to Paul Simon for an extract from *Homeward Bound* copyright 1966 Paul Simon Music.

Strenuous efforts have been made to contact all those not listed in these acknowledgements to ask permission to use their material and we offer sincere apologies to authors and publishers for not including them.

Hunting *Around* the Boscobel Oak

ST. JAMES'S PALACE

Trees play a hugely important, if often over-looked, part in our existence. They provide a strong, light, easily worked and ultimately biodegradable material for every sort of construction. They give us fuel, food, shelter from the elements and habitats for wildlife. At the same time they absorb carbon dioxide and provide life-giving oxygen in return. Yet there are other, less material, reasons for valuing and celebrating trees. They give shape and substance to rural landscapes and soften the hard edges of our towns and cities. Trees also have a unique capacity to lift our spirits and it is this entirely intangible dimension that Piers Browne evokes so splendidly in the book.

For me, the most memorable glimpses of trees have as much to do with the quality of the light as with the trees themselves. Whether it is the steely glint of winter sun on the bark of an elderly oak, the first fresh green leaves of a birch in spring, the sculpted blue-green canopy of a Scots Pine in summer, or the solid glow of an autumnal beech, it is the interplay with the light that fixes the image in the mind. This straightforward beauty is matched by a mysterious, haunting aura that surrounds more ancient trees. How long have they been there? What sights have they seen? What interesting people have passed them by, or sat at their feet? Both the beauty and the mystery of trees have the capacity to stir our emotions, and are captured in this book.

In today's world, with its ever-shorter time horizons and insistent demands for 'efficiency', safeguarding our trees and encouraging their regeneration are not easy tasks. Yet it is hard to think of another way in which our generation can make such a direct contribution to the spiritual refreshment and well-being of our successors for hundreds of years to come. I hope that Piers Browne's work, together with the prose and verse that he has chosen to accompany it, and Professor Bellamy's illuminating descriptions, will provide powerful encouragement for taking such a long-term view.

INTRODUCTION

THE TIME LORDS, GREAT TREES IN THE LANDSCAPE AND PSYCHE OF GREAT BRITAIN

Four score years and ten are but a twinkling in the time scale of life upon this Earth, while 3.6 billion is just too long for us even to contemplate. Perhaps that is why we, mere mortals, have so long stood in reverence of trees, each one a pillar of knowledge stretching up to the cathedral of the skies while casting their cooling ombrage of wisdom over the panoply of life.

Today the clever modern men of science can read the story of their lives writ small in every trunk and every wetland that stores carbon as wood or peat cooling the brow of this our suffering, blue-green planet, our spaceship Earth fevered by people who care more for self than for the selfless trees.

Each tree trunk is made of millions of long, thin woody elements. These once living cells gave their lives in the call of duty, their lot not only to carry life-giving water from roots to leaves but to store megabytes of environmental information laid down in their rings of growth, season by season, year by year. Viewed beneath a microscope, the width and luxuriance of these elements of truth tell how good each season was at producing the cells that gave life to the tree and strength and lasting beauty to its wood - Mother Nature's own renewable organic resource, a plastic without equal.

Each trunk, whether still growing, preserved in a medieval building, a prehistoric burial mound or a peat swamp, is a time-capsule of intricate information concerning our ever-changing climate. As it grows in girth, being weather-wise, it is a self-recording barometer of the past and is the litmus of environmental change. Collate all the information stored on these hard discs together and you have an age-old database detailing the vagaries of the global greenhouse, at least over the timescale of what I would like to call the Time Lord Trees.

Like all living things, the Time Lords revel in the act of procreation, each sending millions of pollen grains free on the wind or by special messengers, insects, birds, bats and even small mammals, go-betweens in an annual orgy of free love. Each is a grain of paternal truth concerning its lineage and is suffused with hormones which add the joy of sex to this necessary (the prudish might still say evil) act of reproduction. All pollen grains wear a sculptured sheath, a fingerprint of its own kind, and wherever those unlucky in love fall celibate upon wet earth beneath, perversely they

[xiii]

record the reproductive success of their luckier kith and kin set against the changing climate. Each peat or silt deposit is thus a book that records the history of the Time Lord Trees, there to be interpreted with all the care that it deserves.

This great book is one man's interpretation of the wisdom of the Time Lords here in Britain, crafted at a time when destruction of their ancient world has reached a suicidal rate.

THE GLORIOUS TREES OF GREAT BRITAIN

Oaks THE HEART AND SOUL OF THE BRITISH LANDSCAPE

PIERS Browne was a Shropshire lad brought up in a house that was partly made of recycled naval ships of the Hearts of Oak armada line. It stands upright to this day still held together with wooden plugs which even the rust of ages seems unable to corrupt. Little wonder then that you will find the soul of Britain crafted into the pages of this book, for this is a man who can see both the wood and the trees together in all their glory.

Our native oaks returned to Britain after the last Ice Age some ten thousand years ago, stalwarts in the process of succession which healed the terrain shattered by ice and frost. They added their own substance to the landscape as they helped make and hold the rich soils of England, Scotland and Wales. Be we of Celtic, Roman, Saxon, Norman or other local stock, our ancestors evolved within the kingdom whose landscapes were ruled by oaks - *quercus* their generic name. Shade they cast in plenty, but the effect of their presence was more all-embracing: the atmosphere itself became heavy with an *effleurage* of the special chemicals that, distilled from the summer canopy of leaves and the rich mulch of winter litter, gave Britain's unique natural background a homeopathy of healing chemicals which some believe help regulate our own internal chemistry and hence our lives. It is a remedy which changes with the seasons.

The sleep of winter lets the fungi of damp decay reign supreme, recycling everything that is needed for another joyous year. Spring's birth unfolds all buds that shine with protective resins as flowers come into bloom and leaves unfold. Summer matures and a multitude of insects do their worst leaving the leaves in tatters despite the whole *armamentarium* of protective chemicals they produce. In August comes the oaks' own special season of Lammastide when each great tree produces a new crop of soft luscious leaves to feed the insect larvae ready for their winter sleep, and thus heralds autumn, a time of hurried plenty for both the trees and their dependents who must stock up for the winter. At this time the goodness in the green of chlorophyll is recycled to reveal the many splendoured tints of autumn until again back to the well-earned rest of winter.

The same is true for all our deciduous Time Lord Trees, which along with their evergreen cousins play a high-rise

The Long Walk to Windsor Castle

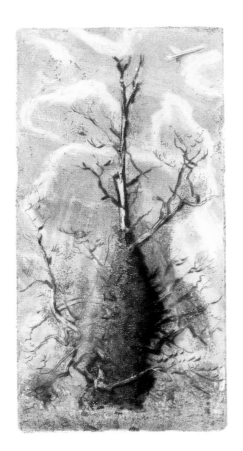

role in the way of life that is quintessentially British. You can take a man away from the bogs of Ireland but you can't take the bog from the man! The same is true of the oaks of Britain which have been revered as sacred trees across Europe: Maximus of Tyre wrote of the Celts worshipping the oak as a symbol of Zeus, the God of thunder, in the second century AD; oaken ashes or charcoal are often found associated with prehistoric cremations; for many centuries herbalists preferred to use mistletoe and polypody fern found growing on oaks believing that it was suffused by the virtues of the tree, and the *geanncanach* or leprechaun of the Irish smoked pipes made of acorns. Here, 29 May became 'Oak Apple' or 'Shick-Shack Day' celebrating the fact that Charles II found refuge in an oak at Boscobel after the Battle of Worcester. The shick-shack, a piece of oak with an oak apple, was worn in Oxfordshire before noon, to be replaced by 'monkey powder', ash leaves, in the afternoon. If either was worn in the evening the miscreant of custom would be beaten with nettles.

William Borlase's *Natural History of Cornwall* printed in 1758 tells the following story concerning Charles I who set up his standard in an oak tree in Boconnoc Park at the Battle of Braddock Down. After his 'murder' the leaves of that great oak suddenly changed white, and remained so for thirty years. The green man who appears in carvings in many places of worship from the humblest of parish churches to the most magnificent of our cathedrals is often swathed in oak leaves. So deeply is the oak steeped in the mythology of our people that, despite the fact there are two species, oak is the only common name used across the length and breadth of these fair islands. The same is true in wider context, for the Latin word *quercus* also means 'tree'.

Whether the pedunculate oak (*quercus robur*), with its long stalked acorns, or sessile oak (*quercus petrea*), which has neither of these distinguishing features, these great trees are not only of importance to people but also to the insects and other creeping crawling things. So crucial as nature reserves are our oaks for these critically important members of the living world that these lone patriarchs now have official protection as Sites of Special Scientific Interest.

THE pollarded oak is smeared with creosote,
its cropped head on fire with mistletoe like smoke;
a red seal for every limb removed
and for every scar a new spike in the crown.
Wounds drive the roots deeper,
out like spokes to the hill's rim.
What we cannot hold we destroy, or attempt to destroy.
But the horned god carries cautery like a flag.

ROBIN ROBERTSON from HILL FORT

Pollard Oaks, Knebworth

'The girt woak tree that's in the dell! Ther's noo tree I da love so well' as the Dorset vicar-poet William Barnes wrote in the mid-nineteenth century, could apply to this secretive rather stumpy Salopian one seen here on a sunny but breezy June afternoon. A holly bush happily grows about ten feet up beneath five massive branches radiating from the sturdiest, most solid trunk the artist has ever seen. The Lydham tree, unlike some famous hollow-trunked oaks such as the Bowthorpe oak just off the A1 in Lincolnshire whose age has been proposed as being over a thousand years, has a girth of about forty feet, exactly the same as the Bowthorpe oak. But unlike the Bowthorpe or Major oaks, the Lydham's healthy limbs grow happily unaided by chains or wires from its middle. Virgil, in *Georgics* II, says it all of this tree:

> Deep in the bowels of the earth, the oak
> With hardy effort drives his vigorous root:
> And rears his head as high. No winter storm
> Can touch a trunk so founded. Years revolve;
> The puny generations of mankind,
> Each after each, expire; yet firm he stands;
> And stretching, far and wide, his sinewy arms,
> With comprehensive span, and sweep of shade,
> O'er spreads a district.

[4]

THE trees were the worst loss and damage, for at Sharkey's bidding they had been recklessly cut down far and wide over the Shire; and Sam grieved over this more than anything else. For one thing, this hurt would take a long time to heal, and only his great-grandchildren, he thought, would see the Shire as it ought to be.

Then suddenly one day, for he had been too busy to give a thought to his adventures, he remembered the gift of Galadriel. He brought the box out and showed it to the other Travellers (for so they were now called by everyone), and asked for their advice.

'I wondered when you would think of it,' said Frodo. 'Open it!'

Inside it was filled with a grey dust, soft and fine, in the middle of which was a seed, like a small nut with a silver shale. 'What can I do with this?' said Sam.

'Throw it in the air on a breezy day and let it do its work!' said Pippin. (...) So Sam planted saplings in all the places where specially beautiful or beloved trees had been destroyed, and he put a grain of the precious dust in the soil at the root of each. He went up and down the shire in this labour.

(...)

Spring surpassed his wildest hopes. His trees began to sprout and grow, as if time was in a hurry and wished to make one year do for twenty.

J. R. R. TOLKIEN from THE LORD OF THE RINGS, BOOK SIX, VIII

Massacring Arden's Oaks: building the M42

The young Tolkien was inspired by oaks in the Forest of Arden to think of it later as hobbit land. Shakespeare, born nearby, probably chose it as the setting for *As You Like It*. Once part of a large forest, the Forest of Arden (arden was an old British word signifying a wood) was half of Warwickshire. The Arden area is south-west of Birmingham with the M42 bisecting it just as the M3 dissects Twyford Down. In both places woods have been hopelessly wittled away.

May Midday: Chestnut Leaved Oak in Kew Gardens

ALL the space in the world to grow,
a somnolent and drowsy air
at Kew.
There immigrants from all the earth
are loved and nourished from seed-birth
and thrive.
Pampered prey in wizards' hands,
this Persian guest with rich dark leaves
sharp cut with laserfine relief
grows fat.

This is luckily a pampered oak because, due to the steady drying out of the soil at Kew, a dryness compounded by the compacting of the soil above its roots by the trampling of many hard-soled shoes, the nitrogen depleted earth around its roots is now being aerated in the usual way of pumping compressed air (air is seventy-eight per cent nitrogen) or even something more exotic like nitrous oxide down amongst them. However it is to be seen whether this vast and lovely tree will be saved.

MARGARET WHYTE

Holm Oak, Dyrham Park: May Evening

My God, when I walk in those groves,
And leaves thy spirit doth still fan,
I see in each shade that there grows
An angel talking with a man.

Under a juniper, some house,
Or the coold myrtle's canopy,
Others beneath an oak's green boughs,
Or at some fountain's bubbling eye ...

HENRY VAUGHAN from RELIGION

[7]

Cork Oak

Despite the proximity of warming sea, at between 54 and 55 degrees latitude, this rare cork oak in the churchyard of St Mary's, Gosforth has done well to survive. The church is highly important having two ancient hogback tombs, one of a Viking chief, 'The Warrior's Tomb', and the other, 'The Saint's Stone' possibly containing one of our first church leaders well before 1066, and the last of four tall Viking stone crosses in its church-yard. Made around 940AD, the cross, so well showing the perfect fusion between Viking myth and Christian belief, is fourteen and a half feet high. Its lower, round part represents the ash tree *yggrasil*, which Norsemen believed supported the universe, while the square-sided top portion before the cross shows scenes from the Voluspa, a Norse saga describing the creation and the end of the world. The Saint's Tomb has carved on it both the last great battle in Norse saga and a crucified Christ at either end.

PENNED in a northern graveyard far from Iberian kin
a cork oak, bent as an ancient three pronged fork,
stays where some arborialist has digged it in.

The western wind has flogged it to its knees
and made it join the dead as they face east.
It keeps its tears, its leaves, its precious cork
and sends its roots to rive a buried feast.

MARGARET WHYTE

[8]

Wistman's Wood, Dartmoor – with Stonechat

In 1620, Tristram Risdon wrote of this distictive but small wood huddling to the side of a gulley on Dartmoor near Postbridge:

The trees were no taller than a man may touch his head.

Although they have grown about seven times since then to a height of twenty feet, in 1912 a geological survey team had attempted to work in the wood but gave up after a few hours because the spreading boughs over rocks made walking well nigh impossible. Their difficulty was the very thing which has until the present day preserved intact from man's industry a gnarled and moss covered little wood.

Sᴏᴍᴇᴛʜɪɴɢ is in the wood but nothing
visible. Continuance; a filmy, brackish
misting of oak and moss,
cold as the shilling minted in the frost
winking at break of day through dusted grass:
a faery money, changing in our hands
to silverthaw.

JOHN BURNSIDE: SOMETHING IS IN THE WOOD

[9]

White Sails: Red Oak, Blonde Girl: Helford Estuary

THE solitary yachtsman who leaves his yacht in an open roadstead in Helford, and goes exploring up-river in his dinghy on a night in midsummer, when the nightjar calls, hesitates when he comes upon the mouth of the creek, for there is something of a mystery about it even now, something of enchantment. Being a stranger, the yachtsman looks back over his shoulder to the safe yacht in the roadstead, and to the broad waters of the river, and he pauses, resting on his paddles, aware suddenly of the deep silence of the creek, of its narrow twisting channel, and he feels - for no reason known to him - that he is an interloper, a trespasser in time.

DAPHNE DU MAURIER *from* FRENCHMAN'S CREEK

The Ash

In the North, the place of the oak is taken by the ash, for the people of the harsher climates have become linked to this Time Lord above all others. It grows fast and can outlive the oak. Its divided, compound leaves cast but a light shadow and so allow a diverse flora to grow on the rich mulch soils they help to create. Ash glades attract the game to feed. Well-lit, they are places of easy quarry, fast food for those whose only source of sustenance was to hunt and gather the richness of the forests. The same was of course true for the trees themselves for their soft leaves are the first to be drawn underground by worms, and so the goodness they contain are rapidly turned to humus that holds the minerals safe ready to charge the sap as it rises in the spring of another year. It was the favourite timber for fuelling fires, as it will burn well while still green.

In Norse mythology the ash is 'yggdrasill', the Great World Tree and the strong axis around which the three planes of existence revolve and in whose roots dwell the serpent of infinite libido. A goat, which fed on the leaves, gave milk to the heroes of Valhalla, and at the moment of destruction of the world this tree became a guardian mother regenerating a whole new race of people. The Vikings built their boats and made the shafts of their spears from its strong wood. The Anglo-Saxon word for 'battle' comes from *aese-plega*, the 'game of spears'. Mothers hung their cradles from its branches seeking protection for their babies from evil spirits. Its use in medicine and magic are legion: on Christmas Eve the burning of an ashen faggot was a popular fire charm ceremony in inns and farmhouses, helping maidens to find their swain when nothing was luckier than an 'even as', an even number of these pinnate leaves - thirteen being our common or European ash's norm prior to any conflagration.

In his *Natural History of Selborne*, Gilbert White tells of ashes which had been left with clefts held open by wedges through which a ruptured child was passed stark naked. The tree was then plastered with loam and well swathed up. Variants of this traditional cure were in use in Devonshire as recently as 1902. When the child's father was asked why he had gone through this ritual, he seemed surprised and said: 'Why, all folk do it!' White also tells of another Selborne superstition: if shrews, which were also known as 'fairy mice' ran over the cattle and stiffened their limbs, the cure was to stroke their backs with a branch from a 'shrew ash' - a special tree into which a hole had been augured and a living shrew had been entombed with a plug of wood.

Ash Grove

THE even ash-leaf in my left hand,
The first man I meet shall be my husband.
The even ash-leaf in my glove,
The first I meet shall by my love.
The even ash-leaf in my breast,
The first man I meet's whome I love best.
The even ash-leaf in my hand,
The first I meet shall be my man.
Even ash, even ash, I pluck thee,
This night my true love for to see;
Neither in his rick nor in his rear,
But in the clothes he does every day wear.
Find even ash or four-footed clover,
An' you'll see your true love before the day's over.   TRADITIONAL

[13]

Upper Lambourn

Up the ash-tree climbs the ivy,
Up the ivy climbs the sun,
With a twenty-thousand pattering
Has a valley breeze begun,
Feathery ash, neglected elder,
Shift the shade and make it run -

Shift the shade towards the nettles,
And the nettles set it free
To streak the stained Carrara headstone
Where, in ninety-twenty-three,
He trained a hundred winners
Paid the final entrance fee.

Leathery limbs of Upper Lambourn,
Leathery skin from sun and wind,
Leathery breeches, spreading stables,
Shining saddles left behind -
To the down the string of horses
Moving out of sight and mind.

Feathery ash in leathery Lambourn
Waves above the sarsen stone,
And Edwardian plantations
So coniferously moan
As to make the swelling downland,
Far-surrounding, seem their own.

JOHN BETJEMAN

Blacksmith's Backyard, Upper Lambourn

Weeping Ash: Sleet in December

A cold rainy morning. The ashes opposite are green all but one but they have lost many of their leaves.

(...)

A whirlwind came that tossed about the leaves and tore off the still green leaves of the ashes.

DOROTHY WORDSWORTH from THE GRASMERE JOURNAL, FRIDAY 7
AND SATURDAY 8 NOVEMBER 1800

The Beech

Of all our deciduous Time Lords, beech casts the deepest shade, so deep that little or nothing can grow beneath its canopy. Native only in south England and Wales it has been planted across the length and breadth of Britain both as a windbreak and for the utility of its wood. When the Romans arrived in Britain much of our wild wood had already been destroyed. Without the presence of the Time Lord trees our high rainfall had washed away the rich forest soils, turning their mull to moor, their good earth to the grey earth called podsols common to carboniferous floor covering and in places so acid that only heath, moor and bog could thrive. The peat lands, spreading across mountains and lowlands alike, took down the evidence preserving great tree trunks and the pollen grains those trees and other plants had in vain scattered on the wind. The Latin poet Ovid once wrote two thousand years ago of cutting names on the beech and the names growing as the trunks grew.

In 'mast' years more pollen grains found their lascivious mark, and beechnuts (or buck as it was originally called) paid dividends on pannage, gorging the pigs as it had their wild ancestors in the ancient forests. It is thought that this is how Buckinghamshire got its name, a county famous for its beeches, especially those at Burnham, and also for its bodgers - craftsmen who turned its strong wood into furniture. Bodgers always worked safe in the knowledge that more timber was growing than they used in any year. Their duty of care handed down over generations ensured a sustainable supply of their only resource.

Beech wood lasts well in waterlogged soils: millers used it for their sluices and wheels; parts of Winchester Cathedral, built around thirty-five years before the Norman Conquest, still stand on beech piles - as did old Waterloo Bridge. For a long time beech was not regarded as a native, for Julius Caesar said he had not seen it growing in these Islands, but more modern research has proved that it grew naturally in the South of England on chalk and limestone.

The leaves of the beech are tougher than those of the ash and so hold their store of energy and minerals longer, releasing them to feed a whole foray of fungi that pass the minerals on to succour the Time Lords. Peasant people came to know that they could feed on the fungi, but if bad times forced them to collect too many of the leaves from the forest floor to use as litter for their animals, then catastrophe in the form of acid soils was not far away.

Herb women used the leaves for many things: fresh picked, their coolness helped soothe hot swellings; boiled, they were used both as a poultice and an ointment, while water collected from hollows in the trees soothed sores, abrasions, scabs and scurf on man and beast. So too the housewife collected autumn leaves to provide fragrant stuffing in mattresses: lasting seven years, its smell of green tea wafted you to sleep. The catkins were also used to pack round fruit on their rutted way to market, while chips of wood, waste from the bodger's stool, were used to clarify wine, as the words of Abraham Cowley a seventeenth-century poet tell:

He sings to Bacchus, patron of the vine,
The Beechen bowl foams with a flood of wine.

Beech Hedge, Exmoor - with Panther and Pony

Bess in Beech Roots

Leaning back like a lover against this beech tree's
Two-hundred-year-old pewter trunk, I look up
Through skylights into the leafy cumulus, and join
Everybody who has teetered where these huge roots
Spread far and wide are motionless mossy dance,
As though I'd begun my eclogues with a beech
As Virgil does, the brown envelopes unfolding
Like fans their transparent downy leaves, tassels
And prickly cups, mast, a fall of vermilion
And copper and gold, then room in the branches
For the full moon and her dusty lakes, winter
And the poet who recollects his younger self
And improvises a last line for the georgics
About snoozing under this beech tree's canopy.

MICHAEL LONGLEY *from* THE BEECH TREE

New Year's Day, Burnham Beeches

I WAS hindered in my last, and so could not give you all the trouble I would have done. The description of a road, which your coach wheels so often have honoured, it would be needless to give you: suffice it that I arrived safe at my uncle's, who is a great hunter of the imagination; his dogs take up every chair in the house, so I am forced to stand at this present writing; and though the gout prevents him galloping after them in the field, yet he still continues to regale his ears and nose with their comfortable noise and stink. He holds me mighty cheap, I perceive, for walking when I should ride, and reading when I should hunt. My comfort amidst all this is, that I have at the distance of half a mile, through a green lane, a forest (the vulgar call it a common) all my own, at least as good as so, for I spy no human thing in it but myself. It is a little chaos of mountains and precipices; mountains, it is true, that do not ascend much above the clouds, nor are the declivities quite so amazing as Dover cliff; but just such hills as people who love their necks as well as I do may venture to climb, and craggs that give the eye as much pleasure as if they were more dangerous. Both vale and hill are covered with most venerable beeches, and other very reverend vegetables, that, like most other ancient people are always dreaming out their old stories to the winds,

> And as they bow their hoary tops relate,
> In murm'ring sounds, the dark decrees of fate;
> While visions, as poetic eyes avow,
> Cling to each leaf and swarm on every bough.

At the foot of one of these squats ME I (*il pensero*) and there grow to the trunk for a whole morning. The timorous hare and sportive squirrel gambol around me like Adam in paradise before he had an Eve; but I think he did not used to read Virgil, as I commonly do there. In this situation I often converse with my Horace, aloud too, that is talk to you, but I do not remember that I ever heard you answer me. I beg pardon for taking all the conversation to myself, but it is entirely your own fault. We have old Mr Southern at a gentleman's house a little way off, who often comes to see us; he is now seventy-seven years old, and has almost wholly lost his memory; but is as agreeable as an old man can be, at least I persuade myself so when I look at him, and think of Isabella and Oroonoko. I shall be in town in about three weeks. *Adieu.*

LETTER FROM THOMAS GRAY IN CANTS HILL, BURNHAM TO
HORACE WALPOLE, SEPTEMBER 1737

New Year's Day, Burnham Beeches

H<small>ER</small> father had been a woodcutter, strong as a giant - he could lift up a horse and wagon. From the age of five, when she lost her mother, she lived with him in the woods. They used to sleep in a tent, or a kind of wigwam of pine branches, and while her father was tree-felling, the little girl made baskets and sold them around the village. For ten years they lived together and were perfectly contented. She grew up into a beautiful young girl - 'Some'ow I seemed to send men breathless' - but her father was careful, and when the timber-men came he used to hide her under piles of sacking.

Natasha Drawing in Highgate Woods, London

Then one day - she was fifteen years old at the time - a tree fell on her father. She heard him shout and ran up the thicket and found him skewered into the ground with a branch. He was lying face down and couldn't see her. 'I'm going, Alice,' he said. She clawed a hole with her hands and lay down beside him, and held him until he died. It took twenty-four hours, and she never moved, nor did he speak again.

LAURIE LEE from CIDER WITH ROSIE

THE rain set early in to-night,
The sullen wind was soon awake,
It tore the elm-tops down for spite,
And did its worst to vex the lake:
I listened with heart fit to break;
When glided in Porphyria ...

ROBERT BROWNING *from* PORPHYRIA'S LOVER

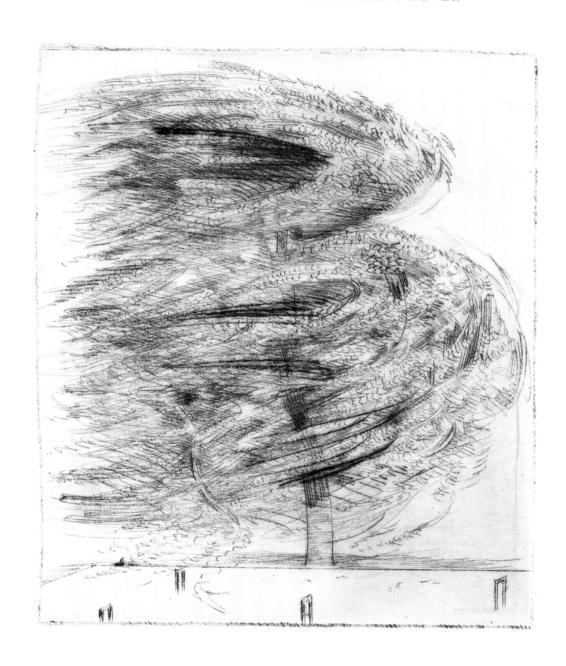

Copper Beech in High Gale

THE Palm House at Kew Gardens was built to the designs of Decimus Burton, architect, and Richard Turner, engineer, between 1844 and 1848. Following major reconstruction completed in 1988, the Palm House has been replanted as a representation of rainforest and features plants from many tropical areas of the world. But come in to the garden Maud and see such wonderful temperate giants as this weeping beech reigning in complementary majesty just outside the hothouse.

Weeping Beech in Kew Gardens

The Dark Hedges

Here, you twisty tunnel of love,
meshing nets of north green snakes,
reaching across a path deep trod
with rooting feet in a hedge of desire;

light and shade deceives the eye.
Once committed the trap is sprung;
Adams and Eves connive entwining
in cardinal sin under groves of fire.

MARGARET WHYTE

The Dark Hedges: Antrim

Beech: October in Beamish

How innocent were these
Trees, that in mist-green May,
Blown by a prospering breeze,
Stood garlanded and gay;
Who now in sundown glow
Of serious colour clad
Confront me with their show
As though resigned and sad.

Trees who unwhispering stand
Umber and bronzed and gold,
Pavilioning the land
For one grown tired and old;
Elm, chestnut, beech and lime,
I am merged in you, who tell
Once more in tongues of time
Your foliaged farewell.

SIEGFRIED SASSOON: OCTOBER TREES

[26]

The Elm

I AM of Ireland,
And of the holy land
Of Ireland.

Good sir, pray I thee,
For of saint charity,
Come and dance with me
In Ireland.

ANON : ICHAM OF IRLONDE

ULMUS PROCERA is the English elm, a magnificent tree that is native only to these sceptered isles. In ancient times, peasants twined their vines around elm trunks; this wedding of the elm to the vine was a favourite topic of Roman poets, a tradition passed on to John Milton:

> They led the Vine
> To wed the Elm; she, spoused, about him twines
> Her marriageable arms, and with her brings
> Her dower, the adopted clusters to adorn
> His barren leaves.

Despite the fact that elm is of all of our native trees the Christian symbol for strength, the mighty elm showed its weakness to attack by a deadly fungus which wiped millions of these trees off the face of John Constable's Britain - and sadly continues its work. The elms had arrived in force at about the same time as the oaks, arriving long before the seas had risen to fill up the English Channel to thus block further incursions by the slower moving trees and their retinue of other plants and animals. From that point on, any trees needed help from the human hordes to make that crossing.

The pollen runes tell the story in great detail with mighty elms reaching high into the sky from Willy Lots' Suffolk cottage in the south to the top of Cross Fell in the Pennines, and beyond. North, south, east and west, this was their demesne, but their nutrient rich leaves, which fed a host of insects, were to be their undoing. The first cowboys turned up on the sylvan scene bringing tame aurochs with them and at first stripped the leaves from off the elms to feed these cattle. Then, with axes of polished stone made in the Langdale factories - long before Wordsworth had put forward the idea that the English Lakes should become a 'National Park'- they set about removing the trees to make way for the landscape the poet came to know so well. This process of change, helped by the warmer, wetter global greenhouse and exacerbated by the burning of the ancient forests, from that time on led to the rapid disappearance of the wild wood. The Time Lord Trees were relegated to serfdom and allowed to grow only in forgotten places or to where they were told. Their trunks burned where they lay and poured carbon dioxide into the heavy air. Later, reamed out by machines that were also used to make cannons, elm pipes carried water into the great cities that sucked farming families from the land. They were also used as coffins for those fortunate enough to afford the luxury - a murdered tree, a fitting shroud for the dead.

Wych Elm Above Nappa Scar

WHAT do you think that tree is on the scar?
It's no good guessing it's a hawthorn afar.
Get closer and see the great block of stone
embedded adjacent to its twisted shinbone.

The west wind and the ice have enforced a disguise
that's uniformed all of the trees on the rise.
The dark shapes that stand, on this still day, so stiff,
include this wych elm dug into the cliff.

MARGARET WHYTE

Wych Elm in Northern Rocks

O<small>N</small> his Scottish tour with James Boswell, Samuel Johnson wrote in his usual resonating and ringing tone after their visit to Iona's monastery :

We are now treading that illustrious Island, which was once the luminary of the Caledonian regions, whence savage clans and roving barbarians derived the benefits of knowledge, and the blessings of religion. To abstract the mind from all local emotion would be impossible if it were endeavoured and would be foolish if it were possible ...

Far from me and from my friends, be such frigid philosophy as may conduct us indifferent and unmoved over any ground which has been dignified by wisdom, bravery or virtue. That man is little to be envied whose patriotism would not gain force upon the field of Marathon, or whose piety would not grow warmer under the woods of Iona!

Boswell also true to his character ruefully wrote:

I had hoped that, ever after having been in this holy place, I should maintain an exemplary conduct. [He didn't.]

Iova means 'the place of yew trees' but due to medieval mistranscription became Iona. (In his sixteenth-century *Life of St Columcille* - Columcille means Columba-of-the-Church - the Irishman Maurice O'Donnell wrote: 'Dear to me is that yew tree:/Would that I were set in its place there.') Here depicted behind St Margaret's ruined nunnery, which stands beside the road to the abbey, is a mature and healthy elm. The Cathedral of the Isles, where the Iona community flourished by still working to bridge the gap between Protestant and Catholic, is nearby. This nunnery may have been founded as a Benedictine house in about 1080 by St Margaret, the King of Scotland Malcolm Canmore's queen, but it was in the first years of the twelfth century that Reginald mac Somerled founded a Benedictine abbey and an Augustine nunnery, the abbey being on the site of that first simple monastery founded by St Columba.

For it was in 563 that, aged forty-two, the Christian priest Columba, exiled it is perhaps wrongly said for causing terrible civil war at the battle of Cooldrevney in Ireland, arrived on Iona with other refugees. By the time he died thirty-four years later, he was revered as a saint and was known as the Dove of the Church and Columkille to distinguish him from other Columbas. He had founded the most influential community in Scotland for generations to come. Doubtless exaggerated, his wonders and miracles, such as vanquishing a water monster in Loch Ness, won over the Picts under King Brude, and all northern Scotland was converted to Christianity by his labours. Iona soon became the burial site of kings of Scotland (including the original and real Macbeth), Ireland and Norway while being the base of scholarship

Dawn on Iona: Elm behind a Ruin with Eagle Owl

and activity: Lindisfarne was founded in 635 by Aidan while that saint's pupil, the Abbess Hilda, founded Whitby Abbey.

On the 8 June 597, Columba was helped by one monk to the top of the hill partly seen in this picture to bless the monastery. That night, just after midnight, he sank down in front of the altar and passed peacefully away. He died almost exactly as the Italian monk St Augustine arrived in Canterbury to do for the south what Columba had tirelessly done for the north. It was Columba's passion for pacifism and reconciliation and his deep love of nature that endure to this day. The start of an anonymous twelfth-century poem called *St Columba's Island Hermitage*, translated by K. H. Jackson, goes:

Delightful I think it to be in the bosom of an isle, on the peak
of a rock, that I might see there the calm of the sea

Pruned Elm: December at Brighton Pavilion

THE painted autumn overwhelms
The Summer's routed last array,
The citron patches on the elms
Bring sunshine to the sunless day.

JOHN MEADE FALKNER *from* EPILOGUE

[32]

COME into the garden, Maud,
For the black bat, night, has flown,
Come into the garden, Maud,
I am here at the gate alone;
And the woodbine spices are wafted abroad,
And the musk of the rose is blown.

For the breeze of morning moves,
And the planet of love is on high,
Beginning to faint in the light that she loves
On a bed of daffodils sky,
To faint in the light of the sun she loves,
To faint in his light, and to die.

ALFRED LORD TENNYSON *from* MAUD

Wych Elm: the Knot Garden, Broughton Place

Camperdown Elm

Is this the only way to make a wych elm weep?
To graft some freak half way up its trunk,
found, vile seedling, by some gothic Scottish pile.
What gross gardener could commit such a crime of style?
Tolkien and Rackham both would be pushed
to conjure such a horror in their sleep.

MARGARET WHYTE

Camperdown Elm: Sunrise

The Lime

CARL Linneus (1707 – 78), the man who allowed the world of science to speak of living things in the binary of a forgotten language, lived in a house blessed by the presence of an ancient linden tree, the symbol of conjugal love and a life index tree for all the family. Hence his family name *tilia* is the Latin word for this Time Lord that when in flower fills the air with a heady fragrance and drips honeydew down upon the earth, while 'x' marks the fact that it is a hybrid, a bastard between two other now less common species - the large leaved lime, *tilia platyphylla*, which is possibly a native, and the small leaved lime, *tilia cordata*, which certainly is. When the Romans rowed up the Thames to found Londinium, Boadicea's woaded hordes were shielded from their view and from their swords by the trunks and the wood of these stately trees, which the Anglo-Saxons named 'lind', linden being more modern usage.

In the words of Matthew Arnold's *Scholar Gypsy*:

And air-swept lindens yield
Their scent and rustle down their perfumed showers
Of bloom upon the bent grass where I am laid,
And bower me from the August sun with shade.

Lime wood has a close grain ideal for carving, as the intricate work of Grinling Gibbons (1648-1721) so beautifully demonstrates. The sounding boards and keys of musical instruments were often of lime. The wood was also used by the aircraft industry: much of the lime in the gorges of the Wye Valley was cut down during World War Two in order to provide plywood used in the manufacture of Mosquitoes, which also spat fire at the Luftwaffe - a Time Lord once again in the service of king and country. Fortunately limes have returned to these gorges, which so attract natural historians, botanists and tourists every year.

Apart from making shields, it found use in great staircases like that at Boughton House in Northamptonshire. There, in the 1930s, the Duke of Buccleuch planted, as his ancestors had done before, a linden avenue to provide beauty, shade and a constant supply of wood to keep the staircase in repair into a fragrant future. Lime walks were planted in many places with their branches trained inwards to form a sweet smelling roof, to form 'brave sommer houses and banketting arbours'. After all, lime was a tree of love. The logs, however, are not for burning for their smoke is anything but fragrant, although in Devon, Cornwall and Lincolnshire its bark was woven into ropes often used for traces and halters.

GOD seed sharp minds that drilled to please
With sinuous lines of tunnelling trees.

PIERS BROWNE

Lime Avenue: Leaves Turning at Clumber Park

This picture shows a fraction of the longest double-lined avenue of trees in Europe at Clumber Park, north of Nottingham, and was planted by the fourth Duke of Newcastle under Lyme in about 1820. Some say it was planted as late as 1840. The original double avenue runs from Appley Head Gate for just under two miles to the main crossroads which would have led to Clumber House, now demolished. Additional planting has taken place at the Carbuton end of the road to commemorate the Queen's coronation in 1953 and later to mark both the seventy-fifth and hundredth anniversaries of the National Trust in 1970 and 1995.

There are large black bands of grease around the trunks to prevent attack by the winter moth which can so astonishingly defoliate limes. Female moths are wingless and would otherwise climb the trunks to lay their eggs in the canopy of the trees. The autumn shows wonderful colour as the limes' bark turns pale viridian and rises from a carpet of orange leaves while the black bands further enhance the smart regimented look. In summer the lime leaves' scent has been called a sweet exudation (Norman MacCaig in *Orgy*) while Robert Nichols, in *The Sprig of Lime*, writes of 'such stinging cloud of exhalation/As reeks of youth, fierce life, and summer's prime.' This is what is so very palatable to bees.

Tree avenues date back to the Persian and Roman empires, and probably represented the idea of soldiers lining a route at attention. Not so popular in the Middle Ages, renaissance Italy saw many avenues of cypress planted, while, in England, lime, elm and horse-chestnut were the species favoured. Eighteenth-century Britain saw, with the advent of the natural style of parkland, the removal of an enormous amount of our grand avenues, a fashion reversed later by such people as the fourth Duke of Newcastle under Lyme. Obviously, the problem of trees dying at different times is exacerbated in avenues. We see today differences in heights of trees in the Churchill Avenue at Chequers in Kent, in the avenues at Hampton Court and at Osborne House on the Isle of Wight where the Prince Consort planted an avenue of mixed species. When Prince Charles first came to Highgrove over twenty years ago, he planted an avenue of limes to line each side of the gently curving front drive - and the summer wild flowers beneath them give a pleasing and unexpected informality to such an avenue.

O, Brignall Banks are wild and fair,
And Greta woods are green,
And you may gather garlands there
Would grace a summer queen.

WALTER SCOTT *from* ROKEBY

On the Greta in May

The Chestnuts

THESE two trees are not native to this fair land but have found a special place in both formal and informal landscapes and hence in the hearts of people. Knowing of its utility both as a staple food and as a sweetmeat and for making the handles for tools, as poles for hops and vines and as staves for the cooper's art, the Romans introduced sweet chestnut into Britain. It became the most coppicable of all our trees. When the first Neolithic axe-man stood back to survey his fell deed, little did he know of the full power of the Time Lords' hidden magic. With the controlling influence of the leading shoot gone, buds latent around the butt began to sprout; they formed a ring of strong young shoots fertilised by the ash of the burnt waste wood. This juvenile wood was a constant supply that could be put to many different uses. Most of the new shoots were felled after a period of between twelve and twenty years to be used to fuel the hearth or as handles for an ever-increasing variety of tools. Some of the strongest were singled out and left to grow to maturity, their ultimate fate to become structural components for timbered buildings, king posts in cathedrals, tithe barns, wind and water-mills, and the bulk of sailing ships of many lines. Each cruck, post or plank is a litany of annual rings, rubrics linking all our pasts to all our futures.

So it was that parts of our countryside underwent a sylvan renaissance in which the Time Lords became stewards in a new bio-diverse and very beautiful type of woodland called 'coppice with standards'. Each stage in their cycle of management provided a home for special flowers and the insects, birds and mammals that depended upon them. Each woodland was separated by flower-full grasslands, meadows and pastures in which sheep and cattle could safely graze, for each was edged with well-laid hedges all set about with trees growing on to useful maturity.

The horse chestnut, with its summer candles of white flowers, was much later introduced from its home in Greece probably as much as an ornamental tree as for any other reason, although, since time immemorial, every herbal bath worth a soaking has contained the bitter essence of the shiny conker that has itself found a firm place in the mythology of the playground. This rhyme of ancient Worcestershire adds sauce to start off the game:

Hobly, hobly ack,
My first crack.

Alice's 'Loveliest Garden': Lewis Carroll's Inspiration, Worcester College, Oxford

ALICE opened the door and found that it led into a small passage, not much larger than a rat-hole. She knelt down and looked along the passage into the loveliest garden you ever saw.

LEWIS CARROLL from ALICE'S ADVENTURES IN WONDERLAND

Flowering Chestnut: *Wales from near Hereford*

LOOKING across the Borderland to Wales
a lovely chestnut in full flower
has no ancestor would have seen
the bitter death of Owen Glyndwr.
Its roots suck deep the limestone soils and shales
where the scouring mountain eagles
snatched the fatter sheep of the lowland leas.

Hunted as vermin to the volcanic rim
the Cambrian tribes, hurdled as traitors
to piecemeal death, died true to their kin.

Once the rich chestnut too drew its strength
from mountains, raised by Balkan fire,
which now sits smug and tight in an easy land
of lazy milk and leisured lush desire.

MARGARET WHYTE

Twilight

It is, and the far woods are dim, and the rooks cry and call.
Down in the valley the lamps, and the mist, and the star over all,
There is by the rick, where they thresh, is the drone at an end.
Twilight it is, and I travel the road with my friend.

I think of the friends who are dead, who were dear long ago in the past,
Beautiful friends who are dead, though I know that death cannot last;
Friends with the beautiful eyes that the dust has defiled,
Beautiful soul who were gentle when I was a child.

JOHN MASEFIELD

Sweet Chestnut: Evening Star, Wiltshire

AN oak or a chestnut undertakes no function it cannot execute.

RALPH WALDO EMERSON

Sweet Chestnut: Killerton

The Thorn

Hawthorn, if allowed, can raise its thorny head more than forty feet to become a stately tree with immensely hard wood. Unfortunately it is usually layered low long before its prime to form an impenetrable hedge. Crat comes from the Greek word *kratos* which means strength, while *monogyna* specifies that the fruit only contains one seed and hence is in strict botanical parlance not a berry but a drupe – fleshy fruit around a stone, like a plum. Greek mythology tells that hawthorn was used to light the temples of Hymen, the god of marriage. Christian tradition links it to the Holy Grail through the story of Joseph of Arimathaea and the Holy Thorn *crataegus monogyna var praecox* at Glastonbury that flowers on Christmas Day and again in May. Never take May flowers of either sort into the house for as they die trimethylamine, the stale, sweet scent of tom cat sex, suffuses the abode.

Both its drupes (hags or haws as they are commonly called) and the young leaves have a pleasant taste which gives it one of its many local names, the Bread and Cheese Tree. Every county appears to have its own traditions concerning this tree, but all sing its praises as a tonic to strengthen the heart and bond with it the many shenanigans that are associated with the celebration of May Day. Bourne, in his *Antiquities*, recounts that on May Eve people of all ranks went 'a-maying': young people would take to the woods to gather branches of may with much music and horn blowing and, with the sap of spring rising in much more than the trees, the love oracle of the sweet-smelling flowers blossomed to the full.

La Beltaine, as the Irish May Day customs are still called, remind us of the true significance of this festival of vegetation and farming: the bringing of summer is celebrated with a May Queen and a May Lord, a maypole and lots of uproarious dancing. Irish belief had it that the sun rose earlier on May Day, that throughout the week fairies and witches were active and that all farm profit would on May Day return - milk, butter and bread could be stolen or bewitched the preceding week! Before the calendars were changed in 1732, the hawthorn was already in full blossom around London on May Day, but it now comes thirteen days earlier although the urban microclimate and global warming may be helping to close the gap.

Hawthorn appears on the crest of the Tudors because at the Battle of Bosworth, which ended the War of the Roses, the crown of the defeated Richard III was found in a hawthorn, itself a member of the rose flower family.

April Showers over Penhill: Wensleydale

Dennis Potter, full of painkillers, talked on television only a few months before he died in 1994 of the marvellous spring blossom:

W<small>E</small> can forget that life can only be defined in the present tense; it is, and it is now ... and that nowness becomes so vivid to me that I am almost serene. Below my window the blossom is out in full. And it is the whitest, frothiest, blossomest blossom that ever could be. And I can see it; and things are both more trivial than they ever were and more important than they ever were, and the difference between the trivial and the important doesn't seem to matter. But the nowness of everything is absolutely wondrous.

The Glastonbury Thorn

Glastonbury, where the winter thorn
Blossoms at Christmas, mindful of our Lord.

ALFRED LORD TENNYSON

Joseph of Arimathaea, the wealthy counsellor who, in the outer circle of Christ's disciples begged Jesus' body from Pilate so he could place it away from the Jews in a tomb near Calvary, was said, on St Philip's instructions, to have brought the 'good news' to England. He was supposed to have brought what the Arthurian knights so eagerly sought, the Holy Grail, that is the cup used at the Last Supper and some sweat of Christ being crucified.

Some say Joseph's visit was all myth, but if not it was on Wearyall Hill just above Glastonbury that Joseph after his long journey from the Holy Land said he and his companions were all too weary to go any further. He then thrust his staff into the ground and from it sprang the Middle East thorn (monogyna praecox) which flowers twice yearly, in the spring and at Christmas. It is a descendant of this tree that I have depicted on this hillock. Incidentally, it cannot be propagated from cuttings or seeds but has spread by being grafted on to our native thorns. Thus it is with due ceremony that flowering thorn twigs from such a grafted thorn in the churchyard of St John the Baptist in the middle of Glastonbury are sent each Christmas to our Queen and once to the Queen Mother.

The legend goes that the original thorn's descendant I have drawn owes not so much its convaluted branches to its exposure to winds but to its association with the crown of thorns Christ wore when flogged and executed. More legend: Joseph was given the Isle of Avalon or at any rate, according to that greatest of eleventh-century historians William of Malmesbury, 'a small island in Somersetshire ... and constructed there with twisted sticks' the first Christian church in Britain, the future Abbey of Glastonbury. Interestingly, Glastonbury was the last abbey to be dissolved, a neat word for sacked, pillaged and mostly vandalised. Henry V111 decided to make an example of such stubborness by hanging, drawing and quartering and then impaling on the Abbey's front gates the head of their sixtieth abbot, Robert Whyting. That is fact, as was the monks' wish through the ages to keep Glastonbury on the map through extolling legends and, for instance, preaching the wonders of Glastonbury's water - which turned Glastonbury for centuries into a holy spa and perhaps second most important place of pilgrimage in Britain, St Augustine having in 597 chosen Canterbury, the capital of the Saxon kingdom of Kent, from which to convert the English. Glastonbury also could never boast an archbishop like St Thomas a Becket (canonised in 1173) or a Chaucer (1340 -1400) to boost morale for all time.

One fact is certain, as the pamphlet available in the church of St John the Baptist in Glastonbury reads: 'The importance of legend is not whether it can be proved, but whether it helps us find the truth.'

The Glastonbury Thorn: Between Heaven and Hell

I WENT to the Garden of Love,
And saw what I never had seen:
A Chapel was built in the midst,
Where I used to play on the green.

And the gates of this chapel were shut,
And 'Thou shalt not' writ over the door;
So I turned to the Garden of Love,
That so many sweet flowers bore;

And I saw it was filled with graves,
And tombstones where flowers should be;
And priests in black gowns were walking their rounds,
And binding with briers my joys and desires.

WILLIAM BLAKE: THE GARDEN OF LOVE

[50]

Fruit Trees

THE first hedges were carved out of the wild wood not only to corral cattle and sheep but to protect the many fruits of orchards. Like hips and haws, apples, pears, plums, cherries and quinces in all their varieties are gifts of one family of the Time Lord Trees. Some are native but others were brought from around the world to sweeten the diet of yeoman farmers and their masters. All are members of the rose flower family and, in drinks like cider and calvados from apples and, from pears, perry have all been tainted with the demon alcohol to produce hangovers fit for kings, queens and vassals alike. What is more, as flowers of all of these trees must be pollinated by bees, the extra sweetness of honey flowed from the skips that bedecked the orchards. The art and craft of apiary not only assured the set of the fruit but added mead to the heady list of beverages that warmed the hearts if not the souls of friars and abbesses – before, in 1536, the dissolution of the monasteries again changed the face of Britain. Wassailing is perhaps the best known of all the tree ceremonies and in its ancient form is a far cry from apple bobbing in a washing up bowl! Then the whole village would assemble with guns, saucepans and all manner of vessels: first they would fire volleys through the utmost branches to wake the spirit of the tree, and proceed through the orchard singing and making as much noise as possible in a party spirit that continued well into the next day.

Mulberry trees (*morus nigra*) are not Time Lords of the rose flower family and they are not native to these islands. However they must have already been common in Britain in Anglo-Saxon times for they sang the praises of a drink called 'morat', honey flavoured with these strange fruits which are in fact a whole mass of tiny flowers engorged with sugary sap that protect the seeds inside. Although the Greek word *morus* is thought to mean 'fool', mulberry is said to be the wisest of the Time Lords for it never opens its buds before the last frost has gone. It is a native of China where, apart from being the raw material of silk, its bark was used to make the first paper in the world. Will Shakespeare, no less, planted a mulberry tree at Stratford-upon-Avon and to this day children sing as they ring around the mulberry bush.

Laden Pear: Christopher Reading

Now as I was young and easy under the apple boughs
About the lilting house and happy as the grass was green ...

DYLAN THOMAS from FERN HILL

Apple Wassailing

The word wassail comes from the Saxon word *haile* meaning 'your health' and was, in England, a Christmas drink, usually of ale, roasted apples, honey and spices served from a large applewood bowl. The association of wassailing and apples has not lost its connection although the term has come to be applied to any kind of festivity, but as usual with much intoxication of beer.

On the 15 January in the tiny village of Much Marcle, on the main road between Ross-on-Wye and Ledbury in Hereford and Worcester, they celebrate apple wassailing. The designated day is apparently the seventeenth, and it is celebrated about this time in most other counties, especially in Somerset as at Carhampton just south-east of Minehead and in a host of Devonian orchards, large and small. That night, the locals surround the largest apple tree and fire blank (and sometimes live) cartridges through its branches. In Carhampton, little pieces of cider soaked cake and toast are placed in the tree, and cider thrown at its trunk. Then, with loud morris dancers, an old wassail song is rendered in diverse fashion, and a toast or three to the good spirits who guard the buds and blossoms. This is to ensure a good crop the following autumn.

Two main things prompt the whole ceremony in our orchards: it is thanking the tree for its cider, and waking the tree up.

[54]

B<small>EHOLD</small> the apples' rounded worlds:
juice-green of July rain,
the black polestar of flower, the rind
mapped with its crimson stain.

The russet, crab and cottage red
burn to the sun's hot brass,
then drop like sweat from every branch
and bubble in the grass.

LAURIE LEE: APPLES

Towards Cullompton: Devon Orchard, August Evening

THROUGH glass through glass we look
after you up the local hill to where
in April rain the first green leaves begin.
The sun is a silver disc and this morning
is lost in a white mist.
It is English weather. Our thoughts sidle. Over
there in the whiteness: apple trees float.

ELAINE FEINSTEIN *from* SUNDANCE IN SAWSTON

Newton's Descendant Apple: Woolsthorpe Manor

One of the most profound scientific discoveries ever made was that which happened on the lawn of Woolsthorpe Manor in Lincolnshire in 1666: Isaac Newton 'discovered' gravity in that on seeing an apple fall to the ground he wondered if the same force which drove it downwards was the same power that held the moon in its orbit around the Earth.

In 1820, that apple tree - a particularly long-living variety called Flower of Kent - fell during a storm. But in 1998 it was discovered that though that tree had been chopped up the original trunk was deeply embedded flat in the ground. So what is illustrated here, and what about eight thousand people come to see every year, is in fact the original tree which has self-grafted itself, developed a completely new root system, and then sprung up again. At 350 years old it is not likely to produce apples and re-enact that scene which would surely have made a certain perhaps equal if more ancient genius shout 'Eureka!'

AND outrageous energies
swarm on the gean tree;
they bend their backs and slowly haul out
the first, the second bud.

NORMAN MACCAIG *from* SPRING DAY

Loveliest of Trees…Shropshire

Councillor Almond's Almond:
Knaresborough at Christmas

T ODAY, the almond turns pink,
The first flush of the spring.....

C DAY LEWIS from FROM FEATHERS TO IRON

The Almond, *prunus amygdalus*, is indeed the first tree to break into spring blossom - in January in the Holy Land. Most probably originally from western Asia (some say China) the tree is, like the cherry, peach, plum and apricot, of the rose family. Words beginning with 'al' are how the Saxons denoted something of Islamic origin - like alchohol, for the migration westwards to the Mediterranean world had occured by 2000 BC when, it has been discovered, the Minoans stored almond oil at Knossos on Crete. Today North Africans particularly adore devouring almonds while we in Britain are the least of all European countries in consuming them. There is a Parisian patisserie that uses three tons of almonds each month! The beauty of the almond is that this, the whitest of fruits, can be eaten while the nut is still jelly in early summer. The seeds can ripen here, but only in the south of England. The bitter almond, which bears white not pink blossom, supplies oil from its fruit, but bearing in mind that prussic acid, the strong poison, can be extracted from it, the Americans have become especially rigorous in their laws labelling items with these grounded nuts in them.

FOOLED by window-glass, Medusa of the garden,
 The one-eyed fruit has turned itself to stone.
Five lashes point, stiffened by more than frost
 In more than silence. Rind compacts to bone;
The tongues are stilled, rose-hips shrink and harden
 A whisper of Pentecost.

But there is something still afire in the twist
 Of trunk and branch whose cadences the mind
Raids for a memory; witch or Minotaur,
 Or something that we thought we'd left behind
In storybooks, but comes back with the mist
 As more than metaphor.

We have to look, but do not want to see the chin,
 The horrid hair, the all-too-likely-clutch
Of what the medlar has instead of claws;
 The bletted fruit that slackens at the touch
Of any weather now. The rot sets in.
 We turn our eyes indoors.

NIGEL FORDE: MEDLAR

Medlar on Crutches: St James's Park, London

THE cross on which Christ was crucified is supposed to have been made from elder. Perhaps, therefore, it is apt that some also believe Judas Iscariot hanged himself from such a tree. After all, the tree is everywhere in Mediterranean regions.

Shakespeare in *Love's Labours Lost* (Act 5, Scene 2) writes with the pun forefront:

Holofornes: 'Begin, sir. You are my elder', to which Biron replies:
'Well followed - Judas was hanged on an elder.'

It is a pity that the elder has such an association since its flowers are so pretty and its ease of finding, and thus yielding of its fruit from our hedgerows for all and sundry, means that many a lay vintner can cheer with its delicious, potent brew. In the past the tree was supposed to offer protection from witchcraft, be a guard against disease and be a particularly good cure for warts. But Michael Hamburger, in his volume of tree poems, *Roots in the Air*, calls it a 'tree-sized weed' and notes its awful smell and lack of heat when burnt.

July Elder: Wensleydale

Spring Orchard, Shropshire

HEARE hills doo lift their heads aloft, From whence sweet springs doo flow,
Whose moistur good doth firtil make, The valleis coucht belowe.
Here goodly orchards planted are, In fruit which doo abounde,
Thine ey wold make thin harte rejoyce, To see so pleasant grounde.

ANON, FROM A MEDIEVAL TAPESTRY MAP OF WARWICKSHIRE,
GLOUCESTERSHIRE AND HEREFORDSHIRE

Milton's Mulberry

IN THE FELLOWS' GARDEN OF CHRIST'S COLLEGE, CAMBRIDGE

In the year of Milton's birth, 1608, was planted this larger-than-life mulberry tree first mentioned in the eighteenth century when it was fashionable to associate trees with authors. Now on a six foot high mound and almost fenced in with its dozen branch-supporting poles, its large leaves and branches are not the originals but are virile descendants from the tree - not, as the nursery rhyme goes, a bush.

Christ's College paid the hefty sum of 18 shillings for three hundred mulberry saplings, and this seems to be the only one left! Although permission was given to sell three on for a farthing, the college was duped like everyone else because James I's desire for the nation's large gardens to each have a mulberry, for making silk from silk worms, was useless because they were sold black not silk mulberries. However, worthy of much pacing around to solve problems or sitting beneath for shade, I bet this tree will still be the welcome focal point in this Fellows' Garden for future generations of students to come - a wonderful memory of perhaps their greatest undergraduate.

Milton's Mulberry: Fellows' Garden, Christ College, Cambridge

A team of five gardeners was keeping the courts and this garden in fine fettle while I drew. (I took artistic liberties to turn it into a nocturnal drawing.) Tourists - and artists and poets - can visit this garden anytime but the holidays - in daylight. When Ronald Knox wrote a limerick about a man thinking it odd to still find a tree in such of a quad, Father Valentine replied with words fitting for a man of Milton's strong faith:

Dear Sir, your astonishment's odd;
I am always about in the Quad
And that's why this tree
Continues to be,
Since observed by, Yours faithfully, God.

*I*lle salubris *Aestates pergaet, qui nigris prandia moris Finiet.*
(A man will pass his summers in health who will finish his luncheon with black mulberries)

HORACE from SATIRE, BOOK 2

Mulberry at Hogarth House, Chiswick

Hogarth, who loved his garden and mulberry out in countryside at Chiswick, died aged sixty-seven.

CREATION might have been like this,
early sun stencilling the leaves
of the first ever walnut trees,
and the cows beside them splashes
of caramel, coffee, apricot, vanilla,
drifting as if under water
in breeze-fractured light.

CAROLE SATYAMURTI: THIS MORNING

Black Walnut, Killerton: Devon

SOME difficulty there is in cracking the name thereof. Why walnuts have no
affinity to a wall, should be so called. The truth is, gual or wall, in the old Dutch
signifieth 'strange' or 'exotic' (whence Welsh foreigners); these nuts being no
natives of England or Europe.

THOMAS FULLER: WORTHIES OF ENGLAND

Rowan, Whitebeam and Service Tree

STAND on any mountain top in Britain and rowan will not be very far away, its bright red fruits feeding the birds that hop the tops as they fly to the warmer south. This Time Lord is equally at home in the lush lowland forests of England and so has many local names, perhaps the strangest being Fowlers Service, not after a famous man of that name but because fowlers used the fruit as bait to attract birds in winter. Hence the specific name *aucuparia* from the Latin *aucuparius* - 'for catching birds'. Rowan probably comes from the old Norse word for charm, for the tree was thought to have power over the evil eye. Rowans are often found by lonely houses in the hills, and Scottish tradition counselled that the cross beams of the chimney were made of its strong wood; likewise on quarter days a rowan stick was laid over the door lintel, another of the ways witches might enter the house. Even more curiously, branches were stuck in the roof to protect it from fire, while rockers of babies' cradles were fashioned out of rowan to guard the innocence of the next generation, and animals were garlanded with rowan to keep them from all evil influences. Churn-staffs, plough-pins, tethering-pegs and horse-whips were all made from this wood, while rowan fruits are full of pectin and make tart tarts and tasty preserves and puddings. How much rowan and timber from the other Time Lords used in the service of Mammon was burned in the Great Fire of London, we shall never know, but, as no one was killed in that great conflagration, perhaps rowan lived up to its reputation, especially as the fire which started in Pudding Lane brought the scourge of The Plague to an abrupt end.

Sorbus is the Latin word for service tree and *aria* sings the praises of this Time Lord in the service of one of its many uses, for it comes from 'aries', a beam. Its very hard wood was used to make cogs for mills driven by water or wind, capstans, winches and all manner of machinery that took the drudgery out of rural lifestyles - until the Industrial Revolution began to cast iron in similar moulds.

Thanks in part to the vision of one John Evelyn, at least in its early days this revolution of industry saw a revival of the replanting and proper management of coppice woodlands as well as the craft of charcoaling. Evelyn, diarist, poet, scientist, gardener and above all a man of the trees, sang the praises of the Time Lords in a most practical way. In his great book called *Silva*, published in 1664, he pleaded with landowners to replant trees on their lands that had already been stripped to provide fuel for glass and iron manufacturing, and they did just that, in their millions. Another great work of his, was titled *Fumifugium or the Inconvenience of the Aer and Smoak of London Dissipated*. A man before his time.

Sadly this sylvan renaissance was not to last, for giants long since laid to rest were now ready for resurrection: in homage to Time Lords that ruled the Earth long before the dinosaurs (whose trunks had born neither flowers nor fruits), men began to dig deep into the skin of their planet to win a new bedrock for their industry. Coal stored away in the depths of vast tropical swamps - the energy of the sun concentrated by gentle giants more than 200 million years before - was there for the taking.

Man in the service of trees, trees in the service of man, we come, in this ring of roses, the whole circle to the service tree itself. A rarity in Britain hidden away in scraps of woodland, it is thought to be a survivor of the wild wood of more ancient times.

The 'London Eye' under construction - sunset 1999 with Plane tree

I SEE all, am all, all.
I leap along the line of the horizon hill,
I am a cloud in the high sky,
I trace the veins of intricate fern,
In the dark ivy wall the wren's world
Soft to bird breast of round eggs is mine,
Mine in the rowan-tree the blackbird's thought
Inviolate in leaves ensneared,
I am bird-world, leaf-life.

KATHLEEN RAINE from CHILDHOOD: THE LOST COUNTRY

Towards the Cheviots, with Rowan

Rowan in Martindale with Red Deer

A ROWAN is like a lipsticked girl
Between the by-road and the main road.
Alder trees at a wet and dripping distance
Stand off among the rushes.

SEAMUS HEANEY: SONG

Shedding Service Tree: Kenwood, North London

Nᴏʀᴛʜ London, stretching out below Kenwood House's parkland, can boast between its made-up paths that extraordinarily bucolic feel which Hampstead Heath, sprawling out beneath it, still evokes. For though near such vast amounts of housing, sloping grassland and woods and its two lakes have given Kenwood's grounds a special fondness with Londoners.

In the autumn can be seen the unusual and striking crimson-pink gleam of *sorbus torminalis*, the wild service tree's large, boldly cut leaves, and this large tree is on a path-side in a reticent corner in the north-eastern area. Yet the wild service tree is one of Britain's truest native trees! Its fruits, when bletted after the fashion of the medlar, have a similar flavour but are not half as tasty. In south-east England they are still known as 'chequers'.

Look at the stars! look, look up at the skies!
O look at all the fire-folk sitting in the air!
The bright boroughs, the circle-citadels there!
Down in dim woods the diamond delves! the elves'-eyes!
The grey lawns cold where gold, where quickgold lies!
Wind-beat whitebeam! airy abeles set on a flare!
Flake-doves sent floating forth at a farmyard scare!
Ah well! it is all a purchase, all is a prize.

Buy then! bid then! - What? - Prayer, patience, alms, vows,
Look, look: a May-ness, like an orchard boughs!
Look! March-bloom, like no mealed-with-yellow sallows!
These are indeed the barn; withindoors house
The shocks. This piece-bright paling shuts the spouse
Christ home, Christ and his mother and all his hallows.

GERARD MANLEY HOPKINS: THE STARLIGHT NIGHT

Whitebeam in Central Ireland

Maples and Sycamore

WHEN the Pilgrim Fathers arrived in the New World, they found the local people eating maple syrup and marvelled at their strong white teeth and their lack of scurvy. Giving a magnificent backdrop to their first Thanksgiving celebrations, the settlers must have also been bewildered by the number of different autumn tints, which included vitamin rich cranberries, one of their first exports back to Britain across the ocean spray. Each spring the rising of the sap within myriad maple trunks provided them with energy to shrug away the problems of a long winter, and each fall a pastiche of colours to remind them that hard times were again not far away. They tested their axes and crosscuts on new timbers of a range of strengths revealing enormous sets of annual rings, some that had already recorded the rapid demise of the great mound building civilizations and their replacement by those survivors who had learned to live with the plenty of the forests and the naturally treeless plains. Sadly those pilgrims were but a vanguard of crosscut sawyers bringing Old World values and diseases to pastures new.

It was the opening up of the New World that started a two-way traffic in sylviculture: the newcomers wanted to make themselves feel at home and to cash in on the rich rewards of the embryonic transatlantic trade. Sadly, as these new trade routes opened up, unwelcome hitchhikers boarded, like the fungus that in two short years wiped the American chestnut clear off the flanks of the Appalachians where it had been the most common tree. The detailed records of travelling plant hunters made science more and more aware of the fact that Europe and America shared a common heritage of Time Lord Trees and other plants. This pointed the way to the now accepted fact that the continents themselves are ever on the move, creating oceans and raising great mountain ranges. So it was that the richness of the forests of America when compared with those of Europe could be explained. The Alps in the main run east and west and so stood in the way of the Time Lords as they made their ponderous way back and forth as the ice sheets of the north formed and melted. Many went to the wall of extinction while, in marked contrast, those forests on the march in the New World, where the Appalachians and the Rockies run north and south, provided lowland routes for the march of the trees.

Sycamore, a non-native Time Lord, was introduced into Britain perhaps as late as the fifteenth century. One reason possibly relates to the fact that it closely resembles

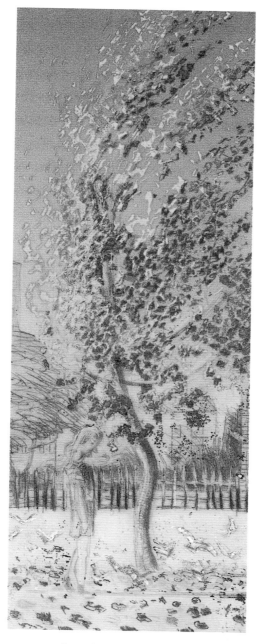

Natasha and Maple in London (detail)

a tree seen by the Crusaders in the Holy Land where it is also called the mulberry fig. Its white wood, which unfortunately turns the colour of nicotine when exposed to the sun, can be wetted and dried time and time again and thus came into its own in the days that laundry rooms featured a mangle with massive wooden rollers. Thanks to the fact that it had 'green-printed' the helicopter long before Leonardo da Vinci stole the idea, it rapidly spread far and wide around the realm.

[73]

WHILE Sandy Lindsay from his lodge looks down
Dreaming of Adult Education where
The pottery chimneys flare
On lost potential firsts in some less favoured town.

JOHN BETJEMAN from OXFORD ODE

OPPOSITE: *Last Sun in Suburbia: Variegated Maple*

Very simple pictures are drawn upon birch bark, indicating by their order the subjects in a series of song-chants with sufficient precision to enable the singer to recall the theme of each in his recitation. An account can be kept of sales or purchases by representing in perpendicular strokes the number of items, and adding at the end of each series a picture of the animal or object to which the particular series refers. Thus three strokes followed by the picture of a deer indicate that the hunter has brought three deer for sale. A conventional symbol (a circle with a line across it) is used to indicate a dollar, a cross represents ten cents, and an upright stroke one cent, so that the price can quite clearly be set forth. This practice is followed in many other parts of the world.

From an unsigned article in *The Encyclopaedia Britannica* (thirteenth edition) on the writing ways of North American Indians - a far later civilised people than the Chinese who of course would have used indigenous paper-bark maple bark as writing pads at some far earlier times.

Paper-bark Maple: Harewood House

SINCE the Field Maple occurs mainly in hedges, some of which are constantly clipped, little timber is obtained from it. Yet the wood is very attractive and takes a high polish, so it is used in turnery and in the making of fancy articles such as trinket-boxes and so forth. In the past it was used for such purposes much more than it is today; the ancient peoples of the Mediterranean prized it very much, especially since to them more trees, and therefore more timber, were available. Pliny (in the botanical book of his *magnum opus Naturalis Historia*) praises its fine grain and attractive veinings. Heavily knotted wood was much sought after, for the knots were usually so beautifully arranged. From it, spotted tables were made, and many of these became famous, such as the maple table of Cicero.

L. F. J. BRIMBLE: from TREES OF BRITAIN

[77]

I'M sitting in the railway station, got a ticket for my destination
on a tour of one-night stands, my suitcase and guitar in hand,
and every stop is neatly planned for a poet and a one-man band ...

Homeward bound. I wish I was homeward bound.
   Home! - where my thought's escaping,
   Home! - where my music's playing,
Home! - where my lifestyle's waiting silently for me.

PAUL SIMON *from* HOMEWARD BOUND

Widnes: Simon's Homeward Bound Station - with Sycamore in Flower

OPPOSITE: *The Gargantuan Sycamore at Drumlanrig, Dumfries*

I'M sick of love; O let me lie
Under your shades, to sleep or die!
Either is welcome; so I have
Or here my Bed, or here my Grave.
Why do you sigh, and sob, and keep
Time with the tears, that I do weep?
Say, have ye sence, or do you prove
What Crucifixions are in Love
I know ye do; and that's why the why
You sigh for Love, as well as I.

ROBERT HERRICK: TO SYCAMORES

OPPOSITE: *Three Sycamores: Easter*

[8 1]

JERUSALEM the golden,
With milk and honey blest,
Beneath thy contemplation
Sink heart and voice opprest.
I know not, O, I know not
What joys await us there,
What radiancy of glory,
What bliss beyond compare.

FROM THE HYMN BY BERNARD DE CLUNY

October Morning Sycamores, Askrigg

Cool Kingston cats loose-leisurely stroll
hot Brixton fluttering red, green and gold;
and joy's out the gutter when colour's unfurled
saying 'Yo!' to lightening our colourless world.

PIERS BROWNE

[83]

The London Plane

June: *The Mall* ('V. J. Day'), London

Two Time Lords were destined to play a very special part in the story of continental drift. They were *platanus orientalis* and *platanus occidentalis*, the American and the European plane. It was beneath a mighty specimen of the former, growing on the south-east Aegean island of Kos, that the leader of the Hippocratic school of medicine penned his famous oath of allegiance always to preserve life. Little did they know that on the other side of the Atlantic a close relative. of that tree *platanus occidentalis* was casting its welcome shade over shamans of another ilk. Separated by at least four million years they had travelled their own paths of evolution and were considered different enough to be regarded as a separate species. However fate would have it that they were still close enough for sexual compatibility. It was either in London or Oxford that by chance their lineages were to be brought back into contact. John Tradescant the Younger (1608–62) one of a father and son team of gardeners to Charles I no less, became the first person to get off a ship with a plane tree. He returned from his travels in America with, among many other things, live specimens of the American plane ready for propagation in his museum-cum-garden-centre in Lambeth. He shared his good fortune with fellow workers at the Botanical Garden in Oxford where the 'Hippocratic tree' was already growing. It was at one of these establishments that the love match was made and a new Time Lord came into being. So amenable was this hybrid to city life with its flaking bark revealing clean white skin beneath even in the sootiest of locations, that it was planted far and wide. Some of the most venerable still grace Berkeley Square: it was perched on the soot-shedding barked branches that a London nightingale once sang.

JOHN Evelyn (1620 -1706) was far more than just a diarist: a royalist who despised the profligacy of Charles II, he worked both assiduously in minor political posts and, with great scholarship, at his favourite occupations, foremost of writing, then of planting trees and gardening, the study of the fine arts and conversing with scientists. He was thus unamused, when his uncultivated lodger Admiral Benbow sublet his house Sayes Court near Deptford to Peter the Great, to find that garden wrecked. The Czar of Russia had found it highly entertaining to be driven about in a wheelbarrow on top of a new holly hedge exactly when Evelyn arrived to pay his respects. The garden was large enough to be given as a public park by a descendant of Evelyn's in 1886.

Called 'the father of sylviculture', it is said that Evelyn instigated the planting of an avenue of planes in Green Park when he was commissioner for improving the streets and buildings of London in 1660. A man before his time - he had done the Grand Tour before it became the fashion - in 1661 he wrote a pamphlet called *Fumifugium, or the inconvenience of the Aer and Smoak of London dissipated*. Of his many writings, next to his Diary, *Silva* was his most enduring and valuable work. Subtitled *A Discourse of Forest-Trees*, it was published in 1664 after its initial delivery to the newly formed Royal Society two years earlier, and contains over six hundred pages with much erudition on every aspect of dendrology and mentions many glorious trees of England. Until the introduction of coke as a fuel, the country at that time was being rapidly depleted of woodland due to the huge demands for charcoal by glass factories and iron furnaces. But it was Evelyn who put in a plea for afforestation and stated in his preface to *Sylva* that he had been able to persuade landowners to plant many millions of trees. Perhaps only oaks now survive that tremendous encouragement from a great conservationist before his time.

Evelyn loved plane trees and in *Silva* wrote that Pliny had affirmed that there was no tree whatsoever which so well defends us from the heat of the sun in summer nor admits it so kindly in the winter. He added:

'And for our encouragement, I do, upon experience, assure you, that they will flourish and abide with us, without any more trouble than frequent and plentiful watering'.

A few lines later Evelyn says he has a hopeful plant at his villa, a gift of the late Sir George Crook of Oxfordshire.

First Leaf Fall: the Broad Walk, Green Park, London

Plane Trees in Minster Garden, York

In autumn, tabby; goldsmith's work and struck
Fire. Then, in the green days, hoisted
Into a clarity of air on endless air.

More than tree, but more than symbol. Can
A symbol stand up to its ankles in earth
And fasten consolations on a tired city?

The Minster shouts 'Eternity! Eternity!'
To the dissolving clouds; sits, cold as Latin,
In English speech of leaves that tell the truth

Of the stone's need, its spring and spread and flower.
A rustle of images in a mind that goes
Forward and back to all beginnings.

We must love to learn echoes, correspondences;
Their failure as well as their aptness,
The heraldry of a world we cannot reach.

We must learn the world is not always where
We find ourselves; but we can get to it.
Today it is a garden in a Book of Hours.

Organ pipes are juggling with Bach,
Unreeling him through shivering grisaille. The trees
Move in a green sarabande: *danse lente et grave.*

Between the arguments of Bach and birds
The bride moves in her own time, stepping among
The planes, lifting flowers to an enormous sky.

She stands in fallen leaves and light and ledger lines.

NIGEL FORDE

October: York Minster from the Close

Silver Birch

LONG before paper was invented, birch bark was used by scribes to record many things from thoughts and mighty deeds to travelling expenses. According to Pliny, the celebrated books of Numa Pompilius, compiled seven hundred years before the birth of Christ and burned with him at the stake, were written on birch bark. His dying moments were perhaps comforted by the resinous nature of the bark, which burns brightly giving off a delicious fragrance. It was for this reason that birch branches and twigs were and to this day are used for smoking ham and herrings and for thatching houses. The multitude of uses for its strong, hard wood are too legion to record as are its uses in rituals of pomp and circumstance. The Romans used birch as a tree of inception during the installation of their consuls, while, as late as the nineteenth century, it was customary on the Feast of the Holy Innocents to beat boys in a ritualistic reminder of the children murdered by King Herod. Birch was also used in midsummer festivals, and in the reign of Edward IV parish records show 'various payments for Birch bowes against midsummer', boughs being transported into London from the country. So important was the birch that at one time a 'besom wedding', in which a couple jumped separately over a birch broomstick leaning against a house, was considered legal.

Of all the Time Lords, birch has been in the landscapes, and hence in the psyche of the people of Britain, for longest for it was the first tall tree to return to these islands after the last Ice Age. Birch provided food for mammoths, giant elk and reindeer, and the wood on which their meat was cooked. Birch trees are among the most hardy in the world, yet in the language of the flowers they are the sign for gracefulness.

Silver Birch: Sunset on the Common

Silver Birch: Winter Sunset on Clifton Bridge, Bristol

CYCLING through the trees we burst
out on to bumpy concrete.

This is where the Dambusters
took off from. Spokes mangle air

as we stand on pedals and
heave our machines into life.

Elbows are wings and the wind
is pretend engines as we

lumber along the runway
like the ghosts of Lancasters.

A tug at the handlebars
and the front wheel leaves the ground

for a breathless moment, then
back to earth with a wobble.

Lapwings, startled from the grass,
flick skywards in eye-corners

and, as we skid to a stop
where concrete runs out beneath

our wheels, fly towards the sun,
touching us with their shadows.

ANTONY DUNN: BARDNEY WOODS

Plovers over Bardney Woods, Lincolnshire

After the Fire: Stoke Common, Buckinghamshire, in January Sunset

THE common still smoulders,
red mere cradled in scarlet sedge.
By searing earth outglowed,
brooding on the edge
the pale sun withdraws.

The Phoenix taps its claws.
A west wind riffles the winey water.
A wing rustles the fired reeds.
Following the minor slaughter
Resurgam. I shall arise indeed.

MARGARET WHYTE: AFTER THE FIRE

Aʟʟ colours are precarious, but yours
Chancier than most. The sun along the hill
Yawns, and they're gone: yellow on yellow, stores
Of distances that shuffle themselves, until

The here and there are both, or neither. Eyes
Trained on summer greens draw false conclusions,
As if your branch-tips in the surly skies
Were ribs of water, merely: light's illusions

Cancelling, conceding, like the flames
Your white logs breed to tease our darknesses.
Vermilion waterfalls, the funeral games
We play to prove the world is what it is,

And that our lives go gracefully for these
UnEuclidean, mad geometries.

NIGEL FORDE: AUTUMN BIRCH

'Lights illusions, cancelling, conceding...' Silver Birch in Wensleydale

A GREENWOOD through a blackwood
passes (like the moon's halves
meet and go behind themselves)

And you and I, quarter-alight, our boots in shadow

Birch, oak, rowan, ash
chinese-whispering the change.

ALICE OSWALD: A WOOD COMING INTO LEAF

Dawn: Birch in Pine Forest

Poplars and Alders

THE lombardy poplar originally came not from France but from America and has been planted widely on the Old World side of 'The Pond'; other poplars are Time Lords of much longer standing here in Britain. *Populus* means 'tree of the people', its trembling leaves being 'likened to a crowd of people and the unceasing course of time'. The Romans believed that the white poplar was formally the nymph Leuce, beloved of Pluto ruler of the infernal regions; when she died he changed her into this tree. According to the Grecian people, when Phaeton son of the Sun, Phoebus died, his sisters who wept for him were metamorphosed into white poplars by Zeus and their tears which continued to ooze from the bark, turned into amber when they fell into water - jewels fit for a Time Lord as they encapsulate insects and other small living things some long since extinct. Today, the black poplar, which gave majesty to the landscapes painted by John Constable, is the rarest, perhaps because it bears male and female flowers on separate trees and perhaps because it produces no suckers. Al is an ancient word for water and *alnus* is in classical Latin the word for tree. It was the Greek philosopher Plato who in his *Critias* wrote of the link between trees and the proper management of our watersheds. He bemoaned the stupidity of his ancestors for only leaving as evidence of their ancient forests the great beams in temples raised in homage to springs which had dried up at the felling of the forests! For the Celts, alder was the tree of resurrection, marking the emergence of the solar year.

The alder has strange secrets hidden in its roots, for it lives in symbiosis, a state of mutual help with tiny living things which began to enliven this once dead Earth at the dawn of creative evolution. In the domain of Ratty and Moley, where the pulse of winter floods have excavated the roots along the river edge, it is possible to see the round nodules engorged with bacteria tethered in the flow. Bacteria in their simplicity can survive because they fix nitrogen from the atmosphere and fashion it into nitrate fertilizer, which is in high concentration toxic to higher forms of life. Alders bear cones and so appear related to the conifers, but close inspection reveals that they are not real cones but ordered bunches of tiny flowers within which the hidden marriage of all the Angiosperms (for that is what this proper name for the flowering plants means) takes place. Culpepper recommended that alder leaves gathered fresh with morning dew would rid the bedchamber of fleas while, placed beneath the feet, such leaves which are clammy to the touch would bring relief to the weary traveller.

[94]

Stableford Mill

No epiphanies at five Crick Road. A damp room,
A greatcoat and a borrowed clavicord,
A two-bar electric fire and *The Woodlanders*.

But one morning I crossed The Parks -
Fitzpiers to the like - for a tutorial,
And centred the Balsam Poplar.
                    And I was Giles Winterbourne,
I was Marty; I was old Melbury, troubled
By the beauty he'd been given.
                    Just the Balsam Poplar,
Slow but sudden, like a bruise. You could find it
Blindfold - the best way on a morning when the mist
Has ducks legs and a roof of sun and thrushes;
Where any tree could be any tree, and I
Was the first one across the wet grass,
Head down among the Metaphysical Poets.

It was the shape of every memory, in translation,
And unique as wallflowers; it gathered in
Old knowledge and new necessity.

Spring: Spliced Balsam Poplar

That one morning spliced the Balsam Poplar
For ever with the century in my head. It is
The bracelet of bright hair, the spider,
Love, that transubstantiates all;
It is Rest in the bottom of the glass; the infancy
Of this sublime celestial greatness.

NIGEL FORDE: BALSAM POPLAR

Out of the golden-green and white
Of the brake the fir-trees stand upright
In the forest of flame, and wave aloft
To the blue of heaven their blue-green tuftings soft.

ROBERT BRIDGES

White Poplars and Pines, Wales

England at her best with gentle, weathered face,
expansive smile, yet eyelines sharply drawn in place.

PIERS BROWNE

Poplars: Hope Bowdler, Caer Caradoc and the Long Mynd, Shropshire

MORNING drains away the ash-white
Hundred-year-old twilight;
The river, spooled by blades,
Is all surface under the light
Leap of a boat from its shadow
To its shadow, shaking
The wet stars.
Lombardy poplars and the juggle
Of darkness; a stir of silence
And a safe day breaking
As eight backs bend
And fire for the perfect centre
Of a bridge-arch meeting water
In a perfect O.
The leaves lift with a regretful sound:
As if, as if. As if
At Metz, Verdun, Amiens, and Bapaume,
The Lombardy poplars
Might have showered some safe
Sunlight down;
And out they'd shoot,
Those blunted limbs
And smashed faces
On short lease, once, to lovers
Of farms at harvest time and girls;
And trees that in French mud
Spoke English. Out they'd shoot,
Whole again and young
And on the Ouse,
Where now the oarsmen slump
Like shot sentries, and the boat
Slides towards breakfast, slides
Across the long, troubled ghosts
Of Lombardy poplars.

Poplars by the Ouse, York

NIGEL FORDE: LOMBARDY POPLARS

Late September Squall over Grasmere: Laurel-leafed Alder

WE walked before tea by Bainriggs to observe the many coloured foliage the oaks dark green with yellow leaves, the birches generally still green, some near the water yellowish. The sycamore crimson and crimson-tufted, the mountain ash a deep orange, the common ash lemon colour but many ashes still fresh in their summer green. Those that were discoloured chiefly near the water.

DOROTHY WORDSWORTH from THE GRASMERE JOURNAL

Willows

WILLOWS - and there are twenty listed in the British Flora let alone the hybrids for they are protean - are members of this family of Time Lords which always grow where water is in good supply. Their Celtic name signifies this, for *sal* and *lis* mean 'near water'. Old English words like *wilig* or *withig* are more utilitarian for they denote their use as withies for ties and in the making of all manner of baskets. Some of the oldest human artefacts found to date are made of willow: sandals, screens, and fish-traps woven out of this pliable wood cut from nature or from osier beds that were later tended with care along rivers and streams. When the Romans started to drain the fens to dig deep into the riches of those black soils, they used enormous mats of woven willow to protect the banks of the dykes from erosion. Some are still in place doing their Trojan work, and more of gigantic proportions are being crafted to this day. Sadly the peaty soils have all but wasted away leaving ever more land below the level of a rising sea. As the peat oxidised, pouring carbon dioxide into the atmosphere, many trunks of Time Lords past and the boats and willow handled tools used by the marshlanders came into the light of day and modern study. Willow wood charcoal was also prized in the making of gunpowder that charged the great punt guns used by wildfowlers.

The Fens were the last place in Britain that the ague held its deadly sway. Long before the New World gave up the secrets of the quinine tree to Europe, the marsh men would collect willow branches and take them to the sickroom to cool the fever. Today we know that the active principle contained in the bark of these often stately trees is the green-print for aspirin, the modern day queller of headaches, cooler of fevers and mediator of heart attacks.

Mythology links these Time Lords to Circe, Hecate and Persephone, all death aspects of the mother goddess. So willow, especially the weeping form, became the symbol of mourning, and in our northern climes was used during the celebrations on Palm Sunday. In the Middle Ages the willow was thought to be a bringer of eloquence, and was sacred to poets. Pollarded willows were often used as markers for parish and other boundaries and their mop-like tops became a refuge and sounding-board for the tick-tock of the deathwatch beetle.

There is nothing more English than a village green, one boundary picked out by pollards, the other overlooked by a church tower, with the sound of leather against willow - cricket bat willow (*salix alba* var *coerulea*) of course.

Wind in the Willow - with Basking Pigs

THRASHING in the grey hands
of the October sky
which threatens to push them under,
the trees fling blue, barbed fruits
at their own reflections
which bounce back with shards of fish
into the struggling branches.

And the gaping silvers,
for one instant, might glimpse
their own image flicking again
in their own element,
an exchange of light like
something trapped between mirrors.
Trees, water, sky, birds, fish

in perfect wrestling equilibrium.

PAUL CARTMAN: KINGFISHER COUNTRY

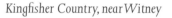
Kingfisher Country, near Witney

Weeping Willow: Radiant Morning, Bath

Leans now the fair willow, dreaming
Amid her locks of green.
In the driving snow she was parch'd and cold,
And in midnight hath been
Swept by blasts of the void night,
Lashed by the rains ...

WALTER DE LA MARE from THE WILLOW

Spring: Osier on the Cam

AND caught once more the distant shout,
The measured pulse of racing oars
Among the willows; paced the shores
And many a bridge, and all about.

The same gray flats again, and felt
The same, but not the same; and last
Up that long walk of limes I past
To see the rooms in which he dwelt.

LORD TENNYSON from HE REVISITS CAMBRIDGE

YOUR health Master Willow. Contrive me a bat
To strike a red ball, apart from that
In the last resort I must hang up my harp on you.

LOUIS MACNEICE: TREE PARTY

Twin Willows, Twin Pekes, London

The Hazel

ALONG with willow and birch, hazel was early on the British scene as the last Ice Age drew to a close. All three Time Lords revelled in the conquest of the open spaces where the young mineral-rich, well-watered terrain speeded their takeover bid. Today, high on the Pennines, the clints and grykes weathered in the limestone still in places bear remnants of these pioneer forests. Hazel is the tree of poetic art for it bears flowers (beauty) and nuts (wisdom) at the same time. Romans used a burning torch of hazel in wedding ceremonies to ensure a peaceful and happy union. This was the tree of Woden, the God of War in Norse mythology; while in Ireland on mid-summer's night, cattle were driven through blazing fires, and their backs were singed with hazel rods. These were then prized for droving, as cattle were booleyed from winter to summer pasture the following year. In the medieval period, hazel rods were always in court, used for the divination of murderers and thieves. In the dowsers' hands the best forked twig for finding water was cut facing east, so the rod caught the first rays of the morning sun.

To ward off bad weather, hazel twigs were worn by sea captains in their hats, and a sprig was said to confer invisibility on the wearer. Cows were fed with hazel leaves so that they produced more milk. In the Midlands a good crop of nuts meant many deaths, 'many nuts, many pits', while both further south and north a good crop of nuts foretold a good crop of babies.

Hazel nuts were also an important part of Halloween for in some parts of the country it was known as Nutcrack Night. Although they did not know it, these pioneering Time Lords set the palynologists of the twentieth century a problem in the interpretation of the history of our woodlands. Palynologists are scientists who spend much of their working days counting the number of pollen grains of each type preserved in layer after layer removed from the great deposits of peat; their dedication is to read and interpret the runes on the leaves of these the first history books of Britain, as we have come to know it. They can recognise the lineage of each pollen grain and from their abundance map the vegetation of the landscapes over at least ten thousand years. All our Time Lord Trees produce pollen in abundance, a sure sign of their masculinity and of the vagaries of the process of reproduction. Hazel is the most macho of them all: dangling fecund catkins that ejaculate yellow pollen onto the slightest breeze, they swamp the pollen record with their prowess. So when all the counting is complete the numbers must be recalculated against the background score of *corylus avellana*.

In Freeholder's Wood, Aysgarth Falls

I'VE left my own old home of homes,
Green fields and every pleasant place;
The summer like a stranger comes,
I pause and hardly know her face.
I miss the hazel's happy green,
The bluebell's quiet hanging blooms,
Where envy's sneer was never seen,
Where staring malice never comes.

I miss the heat, its yellow furze,
Molehills and rabbit tracks that lead
Through beesom, ling and teazel burrs
That spread a wilderness indeed;
The woodland oaks and all below
That their white powdered branches shield,
The mossy paths; the very crow
Croaked music in my native fields.

JOHN CLARE from THE FLITTING

Dead Crow, Live Robin in Hazel Wood

'...But the hazels rose...'

AMONG the woods,
And o'er the pathless rocks, I forced my way
Until, at length, I came to one dear nook
Unvisited, where not a broken bough
Droop'd with its wither'd leaves, ungracious sign
Of devastation, but the hazels rose
Tall and erect, with milk-white clusters hung,
A virgin scene!

WILLIAM WORDSWORTH *from* NUTTING

A GOOD nut year makes a good wheat year.

ANON

The Holly

THE family to which this Time Lord belongs contains some four hundred species mainly in tropical climes: recent study of the lichens growing on holly in the New Forest show species with distinctly tropical connections.

Aquifolium, its specific name, is the Latin word for needle-leaved and its prickles certainly live up to that. Holly, like every Time Lord, is, except in the production of pollen, exemplary in the conservation of resources, and so the prickles are only produced low down on the tree where the leaves could be browsed by animals. Of all the trees, its many spikes attract light to the Earth and so were planted near houses expressly for that purpose; an old Yuletide sprig over the front door was meant to protect the house from lightning. The dark green leaves and red berries both within and without a building protected it from evil influences while making welcome all good elves and fairies. Some also believed that the prickly male holly was lucky to men and the smooth, variegated she-holly was lucky to all females. Not so lucky for the ladies of Tenby in Wales, for early in the nineteenth century custom still had it that on Boxing Day men and boys went a holly beating, rushing around the town beating the bare arms of girls until they bled!

Sadly there is no way of telling a real female from a male holly tree before it flowers, so when planting a new one you must wait until it matures to find out if your garden will be blessed with a crop of red berries ready for Christmas. Lucky or not, when the festive season at last arrives, holly must always be hung before the mistletoe or else bad luck will descend down the chimney on Christmas Eve. For similar reasons custom demands that it must be taken down no later than the eve of Epiphany, a date which in earlier times was given as Candlemas, 2 February. This was twenty-six days later, giving more time for the leaves to dry, for holly branches must never be burned green for fear of death in the family. Poles garlanded with holly were in the fifteenth century set up alongside the Christmas sports, while, in the Forest of Bere in Hampshire, children were given cows' milk in a cup made out of holly wood to cure them from the whooping cough. Ivy was often used in the place of or in conjunction with holly in many of these ancient practices, rites or wrongs handed down perhaps from Rome where holly was the sign of goodwill and was sent as a gift during the festival of Saturn celebrated over three days starting on the 17 December.

Holly

I WENT raving with grief
on the top of Croagh Patrick,
from Glen Bolcain to Islay,
from Kintyre to Mourne.

...

I spent a whole year on the mountain
enduring my transformation,
dabbing, dabbing like a bird
at the holly berry's crimson.

SEAMUS HEANEY *from* SWEENEY'S FLIGHT

Saint Patrick spent forty days and nights on
the summit of Croagh Patrick, so it is said, to
make this remarkable, pyramidical mountain,
that rises from Clew Bay's southern end to
nearly two thousand feet straight from
water's edge, into a major place of pilgrimage
for Roman Catholics from all over the world.

The Comet over Croagh Patrick, County Mayo - with Pollarded Holly

The Hornbeam

THE natural range of this slow-growing, wind-resistant Time Lord is from the Pyrenees to southern Sweden and east as far as south-west Asia. Hornbeam means 'the wood that is as tough as horn', and it was used for all manner of hard working things: yokes, wood-screws, mallets, mells, cogging in mills and as planks for the threshing floor, all taking on that supernatural polish that must be stroked to be appreciated to the full. The tree, which can grow up to more than thirty metres, appears to love the challenge of wind: then it grows in a gnarled and twisted fashion providing groves of intricate mystery, goodly shelter for goblins and murderers or whatever your mind wishes to conjure up. Londoners or any other visitors to Epping Forest should, if they dare, take a walk at night through these witchen groves on Halloween.

Formerly called horse beech, it was once much used for alcoves, labyrinths, mazes, espaliers and pleached hedges. Evelyn praises this tree as much as he did his beloved holly saying that 'the Hornbeam makes the noblest and stateliest hedges for long walks in gardens and parks'. In the south and as far north as Northamptonshire it grows well, and under coppice provides the best of all wood for burning. A twig can be lit like a candle and will burn for a long time. Its charcoal is excellent and the wood is much liked in the bedroom where it diffuses a steady brightness.

It is part of the birch flower family, all members of which bear catkins: the male ones are bright yellow, drooping and up to five centimetres long, while the females are shorter and are made up of several leafy bracts each carrying two tiny flowers with crimson styles. They develop into clusters of three lobed bracts which look not unlike hops with which they were sometimes fraudulently mixed. Despite this malpractice, they make the tree easy to distinguish unless it is another Time Lord up which real hops have climbed!

Gerarde, author of *The Greate Herbal*, speaks of it:

> The leaves are like the elme, saving that they are tenderer; among these hang certaine triangled things upon which are found knaps or little buds of the thickness of ciches (vetches), in which is contained the fruit or seede.

Buzzards over Byland Abbey – with Hornbeam

Ancient British kings and bishops hunted in long gone Cheddar Forest and tried not to ride over Cheddar cliffs! The edge of the tops reach six to eight hundred feet high. Silver hornbeams, as delicately etched here, are especially indigenous in an area far more famed for having given its name both to a world renowned cheese and an extraordinary gorge.

In days of yore, hornbeam was an important member of forests such as Epping (which covered all Essex once) but now, resembling the beech but rarely growing to more than forty-five feet, they are often tamed for use as a hedge or avenue tree, especially in the eighteenth century. Evelyn, who strangely advocated the hornbeam for topiary, said in *Sylva*:

> In the single row it makes the noblest and the stateliest hedges for long Walks in Gardens or Parks, or any Tree whaysoever whose leaves are deciduous.

The Hampton Court maze was originally of hornbeam until replaced by the more usual holly and yew, while the famous pergola walkway in the Privy Garden there, once of elm, has been replanted with hornbeam. According to Linnaeus, the inner part of the bark gives a good yellow dye, but certainly it is used in coppicing today - and always burns brilliantly.

Cheddar Gorge: Hornbeams and Goats, Buzzard and Crows

Dawn: Hornbeams at Brightwell Baldwin

U<small>PON</small> the plaines you shall have ... the Hornbeam

BARNABE GOOGE *in* HERESBACH'S HUSBANDRY

[117]

Pines and Firs

GYMNOSPERM, the group to which firs and pines belong, means 'naked marriage', for in this great group of plants, which include the largest and oldest Time Lords still living in the world, when their lascivious pollen tubes find the mark and grow to their full length they deposit the male principle not into the privacy of an enclosed ovary. Their heritage demands having sex in the raw on the surface of a cone scale. Their seed is not protected and enclosed in a fruit but lies upon that scale whence it is blown forth upon the wind. This is the way of the world for the Time Lords that bear cones not flowers. There are only four conifers native to these isles: juniper, pine, larch and yew. The rest that today cover so much of Britain were introduced mostly from similar climates around the world, first for curiosity then for amenity and utility.

As Britain stood shaken but victorious at the end of the First World War, the Prime Minister, Lloyd George, oversaw the writing of a book *The Land and the People*. He realised that in all three principalities much land stood empty of people and trees and that if another war steamed over the horizon we could again be cut off from vital resources, like supplies of pit props vital to the safety of the mining industry. So he set in motion a body that was to rectify the matter which came to be called the Forestry Commission. Great swathes of our uplands were soon covered by the monotony of monocrops: spruce from Sitka in south-east Alaska, 'Christmas Trees' from Scandinavia and other mighty trees that grew so fast that they turned to matchwood when their trunks hit the ground. Mistakes were made: rivers ran with more acidic water and grouse and red deer were banished from their ancestral moors. Like them or not, the black woods marched north, south, east and west from arboreta like that at Scone Palace, not far from Dunsinane - associated with Shakespeare's moving Birnham Wood from *Macbeth*.

The promise of timber came to fruition, but the promise of local jobs did not: chainsaws replaced cross-cuts, tractors ousted the shire horse and forwarders did the work of many men in a roar of diesel fumes. Over sixty years on, as the first crops began to mature, things began to change, and that irascible Welshman's dream began to come true. His Commission for a land bristling with trees and brimming with people began to take shape. More than one million hectares of land overflow with trees, while thousands are employed at the Time Lords' pleasure and at least fifty million tourists come every year to enjoy walking through their forests.

First Snow: Pine in Wensleydale

Drawn here in the autumn sensibly, as winters at this famous arboretum in the inland, southern part of Scotland near Peebles can be ruthlessly cold, Dawyck, with Scrape Glen in its centre, is where to see both variety and extremes of conifer as well as that curiosity, the Dawyck Beech, which seems to have been petrified into a column of wrinkled branches - perhaps due to the chill! In December 1995 the temperature once dropped to -19 degrees centigrade. Rainfall is moderate, about 900 mm (36 inches) a year, so conifers from the moist and relatively mild west coast of North America, such as the 'big tree' or Sierra redwood (*siquoiadendron giganteum*), Western hemlock (*tsuga heteophylls*) and Douglas fir, grow slower here than in the west of Scotland. Eastern hemlock (*tsuga canadensis*), from east of the Rocky Mountains, is a good example. Until its top broke, to the left of centre and in shadow in this picture, it was the tallest Douglas fir in Britain; prominent in the foreground left and right are two of these skyscraper Oregon Douglas firs.

Champion Firs: Scrape Glen, Dawyck in Peeblesshire

Pines: Etched, Engraved and Mezzotinted

THEN from the sad west turning wearily,
I saw the pines against the white north sky,
Very beautiful, and still, and bending over
Their sharp black heads against a quiet sky.
And there was peace in them; and I
Was happy, and forgot to play the lover,
And laughed, and did no longer wish to die;
Being glad of you, O pine-trees and the sky!

RUPERT BROOKE: PINE TREES AND THE SKY: EVENING

Thinking of the annual gift from Norway to central London and thus the sacrifice of a common or Norway spruce reminds one of Sydney Carton's thoughts on the guillotine's scaffold in Paris:

It is a far, far better thing that I do, than I have ever done; it is a far, far better rest that I go to, than I have ever known.

CHARLES DICKENS from A TALE OF TWO CITIES

The Norwegian Tree and Skaters: Trafalgar Square

Hot Silence

THE serpent-rooted pine-trees, row on row,
Just as they stood a thousand years before,
Rise up innumerable along the shore.
Their glittering cones fleck the white sand below.

CLIFFORD BAX

Newborough Forest, South-East Anglesey

One can see and hear in evenings how this large pine forest in the 'new borough' has curiously become the adopted home of a massive population of ravens. In 2000 there were about two thousand! They do not mate and breed in the wood but journey - and they are great travellers - to the cliffs and mountains of Ireland, Scotland and nearby Snowdonia. They take about an hour to fly to Ireland where, as usual, they feed on carrion. An intelligent bird, once thought of as evil because of their blackness and vast beaks, they can live up to fifty years but usually expire before their twentieth. It is thought they mate for life.

Some Trees

THESE are amazing: each
Joining a neighbor, as though speech
Were a still performance.
Arranging by chance

To meet as far this morning
From the world as agreeing
With it, you and I
Are suddenly what the trees try

To tell us we are:
That their merely being there
Means something; that soon
We may touch, love, explain.

And glad not to have invented
Some comeliness, we are surrounded:
A silence already filled with noises,
A canvas on which emerges

A chorus of smiles, a winter morning.
Place in a puzzling light, and moving,
Our days put on such reticence
These accents seem their own defence.

JOHN ASHBERY

Sunset on Bark: in the Pinetum, Scone Palace

My Cathedral

Like two cathedral towers these stately pines
Uplifted their fretted summits tipped with cones;
The arch beneath them is not built with stones,
Not Art but Nature traced these lovely lines,
And carved this graceful arabesque of vines;
No organ but the wind here sighs and moans,
No sepulchre conceals a martyr's bones,
No marble bishop on his tomb reclines.
Enter! the pavement, carpeted with leaves,
Gives back in softened echo to thy tread!
Listen! the choir is singing; all the birds,
In leafy galleries beneath the eaves,
Are singing! Listen, ere the sound be fled,
And learn there may be worship without words.

HENRY LONGFELLOW

OPPOSITE: *Wellingtonia and Douglas Firs: Dawn in Scone Pinetum*

WHEN we commence to draw or paint a scene, we must first arrive at some form of scale for the picture, whether by experience or by deliberate thought ...

The relationship between the station point, the position of the baseline of the picture and the distance of that part of the ground plane it represents is shown in Fig. 90a. S is the station point and PP1 the picture plane. The horizon line H is shown where a horizontal line from S meets the picture plane. Point A represents the base of the proposed picture at a position half-way between the horizon line and the ground plane. If a line is now drawn from S through A to meet the ground plane at A1, it will be found that P1A1 is equal to S1P1, or that if HA is half HP1, then S1A1 is twice S1P1, because AP1 and SS1 are parallel and sides of similar triangles. Similarly, if HB is 1/3 HP1, then S1B1 is equal to three times S1P1. From this it can be concluded that the ratio of HA or HB to SS1 is the same as S1P1 to S1A1 or S1B1, or that

$$\frac{HA}{SS1} = \frac{S1P1}{S1A1}$$

A. F. HOLLIS from PERSPECTIVE DRAWING

Leylandii in Lincolnshire with Swans

LEYLANDII is a relatively recent phenomenon. It was first raised in 1888, a hybrid not between brother and sister species in the same genus, but between plants from two completely different genera. It is a genuine bastard.

The Monterey cypress (*cupressus macrocarpa*) was crossed with the Nootka false-cypress (*chamaecyparis nootkatensis*), both North America trees, to produce a new intergeneric hybrid. The ignominy of its birth was overlooked until 1926, when it was first given the name *cupressus leylandii*.

STEPHEN ANDERTON from THE TIMES, 11 AUGUST 2000

SAD handfuls of green air
Hang in the gloom. The sun
Nails tatters of foxfur
On the bark of larch and fir.

NORMAN MACCAIG *from* FIREWOOD

Larch in March: Dawn on the Common

I Remember, I Remember

I REMEMBER, I remember
    The fir trees dark and high;
I used to think their slender tops
    Were close against the sky:
It was a childish ignorance,
    But now 'tis little joy
To know I'm farther off from Heaven
    Than when I was a boy.

THOMAS HOOD

The Noblest Noble in England: Millichope Park

THEY shall be accounted poet kings
Who simply tell the most heart-easing things.

JOHN KEATS *from* SLEEP AND POETRY

Scots Pine at Rothiemurchus

THE branches of the Chilean pine are like snakes partly coiled around the trunk, and stretching forth their long slender bodies in quest of prey.

JOHN CLAUDIUS LOUDON

Loudon was a Scottish horticulturalist whose enormous studies resulted in many works on horticulture including his *Encyclopaedia of Gardening* of 1822. However it was a simple Cornishman of that time whose words were immortalised when he said of the pine that 'it would puzzle a monkey to climb the tree!' In mythology this pine brought bad luck, but when introduced into Britain in 1796 it attracted enormous interest - and the Victorians were like today's Belgians in having one in almost every garden! The instigator of this was Menzies, the famous botanist who accompanied, in that capacity, Captain George Vancouver on his voyages along the Chilean coast. Menzies presented some of the seeds he had collected to the Royal Botanic Gardens in Kew where for a fraction under a hundred years they flourished. It is ironic that, due to over-exploitation by the Chileans (the seeds are eaten as flour for humans and feed for animals, the wood for building) we here in the UK may send seeds and saplings back to the Andes where the tree is listed as rare on the Red Data published by the International Union for the Conservation of Nature.

Bicton Gardens, near Budleigh in south Devon, contain great timber trees, but the five hundred yard avenue of very lofty monkey puzzles planted in 1843-4 is most famous there.

[132]

THE sea was near at hand, but not intrusive; it murmured, and he thought it was the pines; the pines murmured in precisely the same tones, and he thought they were the sea.

THOMAS HARDY *from* TESS OF THE D'URBERVILLES

Evening: *Weymouth Pine, Dorset*

Cedars

THE most famous cedar in the world is without doubt *cedrus libani*, the cedar of Lebanon, and thanks to its biblical connections it was one of the first specimen trees to be planted in the grounds of palaces and stately homes. The Christian tradition took it as the symbol of Christ and the Jews as a symbol of fragrance, empire and nobility. Cedar is of Arabic origin with Greek connotations, from the word *kedron*, which means power. The ancients of Egypt made use of its copious resin as a preservative in the process of mummification:

> The age long spicy strength
> Of the Lebanon Cedars, shimmering with needles and stout,
> With their perching cones. And Solomon passed to his rest.

This mighty Time Lord, which can grow to a height of forty metres, is a native of the eastern Mediterranean from the Lebanon Mountains in Syria and south-east Turkey. The other cedar that is also commonly planted in Britain is the deodar, *cedrus deodora*, which forms whole forests in the western Himalayas at an extraordinary altitude of between two and three thousand metres. The vast majority of the softwoods grow in the northern hemisphere spanning a whole range of environments from the dry Mediterranean through the wettest temperate regions to the tree line in the Arctic. These temperate rain forests are ten times more fecund than their tropical counterparts, which support mainly hardwoods of great diversity. Along the wettest parts of the coast of western Wales and Scotland similar though much less diverse temperate rain forest thrived before they were slashed and burned into submission. Little wonder then that when the Time Lords like Douglas, grand fir and the giant and coast redwoods were introduced from America they did so well in this wet frost-free climate. The cedars are of course softwoods, for that is another name in common usage for the Time Lords that bear cones in contrast to the hardwoods, which all bear flowers. However such terms of convenience are all too often found wanting: take for instance the fact that the softest wood in the world is indeed a flower bearer from Cuba, called *aschynomene*. With one cubic metre weighing a mere forty-four kilogrammes, its wood is lighter than balsa - with which Thor Heyerdahl built one of his famous rafts. Whilst one cubic metre of the world's hardest, the South African iron wood, weighs an incredible 1.49 tonnes, the so-called softwoods also come in a range of densities with the churchyard yew vying with the heaviest of all.

Cones of Lebanon: Harefield House's Cedar

THE wind in the three-hundred year old
        Lebanon cedars
makes a noise like nothing living.

LAVINIA GREENLAW from LANDSCAPE

Maundrel tells us, that when he travelled into the east, a few of the old cedars of Lebanon were still left. He found them among the snow near the highest part of the mountain.

'I measured one of the largest of them, says he, and found it twelve yards, six inches in girt; and yet sound: and thirty-seven yards in the spread of its boughs. At about five or six yards from the ground, it divided into five limbs; each of which was a massy tree.'

A late traveller, Van Egmont, who visited the scenes of Mount Lebanon, seems also to speak of the same trees, which Maundrel mentions. He observed them, he says, to be of different ages. The old standards had low stems; growing like fruit trees. Whereas the younger made a much more stately appearance, not a little resembling pines. Of the ancient trees he saw only eleven: those of younger growth far exceeded that number. Some of these older cedars were four, or five fathoms in circumference.

WILLIAM GILPIN from REMARKS ON FOREST SCENERY

Morning: the Giant Cedar at Rowton Castle near Shrewsbury

Deodar Cedars: Tollymore Forest Park, County Down

As a man well ahead of his seventeenth-century times, John Evelyn at the end of chapter seven of *Silva* wrote:

'I would further recommend the more frequent planting and propagation of Fir, Pine trees, and some other more beneficial materials both for ornament and profit; especially since we find by experience they thrive so well where they are planted for curiosity only'.

For centuries in the Himalayas the deodar, or Indian cedar, has been cultivated for timber. Many Indian temples and palaces attest to this. It is a tree with precious little botanical distinction from the Lebanon cedar except that the deodar is more pyramidal and thus pine-like in shape. Cedars of Lebanon were the first to be planted over here: Sir Hans Sloane dug in four famous and long-living ones in Chelsea Physic Garden in the mid-seventeenth century which Evelyn saw. It was the Hon William L. Melville who introduced the deodar variety into Britain in 1831 from even further east, from India, and hence later the East India Company imported its wood in huge quantities. The Lebanon cedar was from the outset a lawn and park tree, but the attempt to make the deodar into a profit bearing timber tree over here failed. At the same time the Scotsmen Douglas and Menzies introduced successful, eventually incredible money-making timber trees mainly from the wet mountainous west coastlands of North America although, like Lobb who brought *Wellingtonias* into thousands of large Victorian gardens of Britain from California around 1853, they too found their giants unsuitable for mass afforestation.

Thus paced avenues, like this beautiful curling one at Tollymore near Newcastle on the east coast of Northern Ireland, are for ornament and not for profit. Each to his own: the decorative generals and the industrial foot-soldiers have found their niches.

The Yew

O F all The Time Lords, the yew is perhaps entwined in the heritage of these scep-
tred isles more than any other. All its parts are poisonous to humans and their stock,
except the flesh of the 'fruit' - a word that must be used with care for it is a conifer
and its fleshy cone should be called an aril. Sacred to the Celtic people, it was both
the tree of life and the tree of death, and, because it is almost indestructible, capable
of living to a great age. For the Christian tradition it became the symbol of resurrection. Yew is derived from the Old English word iw, meaning evergreen some say from
this tree itself. When Saint Columba set forth from Ireland, the Land of the Evergreen
Yew (for no less than three of the great Tribal Trees were yews), he settled on Iona,
the Yew Isle. Finally when he made his journey to bring Christianity to the people of
mainland Scotland he landed on the tiny island of Bernera where he preached to a
congregation of a thousand people sheltered under the branches of a gigantic yew.
When Augustine was sent to Britain to preach the Christian message, he was
instructed to purify not destroy the temples of pagan worship, most of which were
in groves of sacred trees or close by springs which the lords of the sacred groves
served so well. It therefore seems cogent to conclude that many of the first Christian
churches were raised beside venerable yews. If the latest round of datings are correct,
then well over a hundred of these churchyard giants pre-date Christianity, five by at
least two thousand years. Add to all that the fact that the oldest still survives at Fortingall
at the Axis Mundi of Scotland - and it could be over nine thousand years of age – and one
is awestruck.

Fact or fancy? Well the fact is that they are there, some in pairs beside the Lych Gate
where they have welcomed the descendants of Celts, Romans, Saxons, Normans,
sons and daughters of 'Britain's bygone bowmen', to baptism, confirmation, com-
munion, marriage and death in the eternal round of life. During the reign of Edward
IV every Englishman and Irishman living in England had to have a
bow of at least his height made out of yew, wych-
hazel or awburne, all local names for this tree
Harold, William Rufus and Richard Coeur
de Lion are all English Kings who died by
the bow. Recent research has discovered a
whole family of poisonous yet healing
chemicals in this tree and called them taxol,
chemicals that are now in great demand for

use against several forms of cancer. So much so that estates with topiaried hedges of yew send their annual crop of clippings for extraction and further research into the virtues of these famous trees. As part of the celebration of the bimillennium, over seven thousand parishes and other local communities were eager to carry on the tradition of the yew: representatives came from their homes to cathedrals, colleges, schools, and some even to services held in the open air to take part in a special act of worship. At the end of it they received from the local bishop or his representative a sapling yew tree that had been taken as a cutting from a churchyard yew which had been alive when Christ walked upon the Earth. Rejoicing they carried it back to be planted in the heart of their community as a celebration of two thousand years of Christianity. Then the miracle happened: many were so inspired that they asked,

'What next? What can we do to help save our environment and our beleaguered planet?'

So every week more and more so called Parish Pumps, people who will act as environmental representatives within their community, are signing on.

Running among the Painswick Yews, Gloucestershire

The Colonnades of Yews: Saint Mary's, Painswick

Irish Yew

About eighty or a hundred years ago as far as I can make out, a tenant on this estate found two young yews growing on the mountains near Benaughlin ... from one brought to Florence Court all the plants in existence originated.

THE THIRD EARL OF ENNISKELLEN TO FRANCIS WHITLA, 1841

Irish Yew at Loughcrew, Westmeath: Mushrooming

Prince Charles has planted one in what he calls the Cottage Garden at Highgrove where it makes a dark pillared shape behind a mass of pale green and pastel coloured flowers. Being female it has berries which are extremely toxic and dangerous especially to babies, so not a good idea to plant on the lawn. It is a very hardy tree and is pollution resistant. Descending from a single mountain-side yew in Ireland - only one of the tenant's yews survived its transplantation - it is beyond the extraordinary just how many millions of Irish yews have been propagated.

As I was sketching one fine day
the yews that grow on Mosedale way,
the mountains in crescendoed mass
above the fierce and silent pass;

the white clouds' roll in aqua sky,
dark ghyll and rocks with buttress high:
the windblown yew, that dangerous tree:
my framework lacks a central key.

The Roman fort lies o'er the Knott,
where Marius' Mules moved at the trot.
Of cold and wind they'd have their whack
guarding supplies on the mountain track.

Not at all remote this hostile place,
home to Rome and subject race.
Two breathless voices reach my ear,
I cannot catch their meaning clear.

Then from the ghyll beneath my feet
two faces nod and smile and greet,
their heavy packs as big as them.
They bob and bow and smile again.

Millennia after Rome's Dalmatians,
these migrants share the destination;
their packs not sized by Rome's decree,
but by the Leisure Industry.

From all the world and still they come,
with boots and maps and packs clamped on,
travellers from the Rising Sun,
and now, guess what!, my picture's done.

The Great Yew: Yew Bank with Scafell

MARGARET WHYTE: THE BALLAD OF THE YEWS AND THE RISING SUN

THE twins were apparently planted in the seventeenth century, by an ancestor of the present Lord Erne, to make a Baroque garden for his castle. Both were cut back in the prevailing style of formal gardening. The twin brother was pruned in the form of a hedge. The twin sister (the one with scarlet berries) was pinioned on a wooden frame and strapped down to thirty-four brick pillars. Under its black shade - more like a dungeon than a summer-house, one would have thought - Lord Erne would entertain his friends.

About 1833, the Lord Erne of the day relented; at least the thirty-four brick pillars were replaced with sixteen oak posts ... Hence the liberated freaks we have today.

THOMAS PAKENHAM *from* MEETINGS WITH REMARKABLE TREES

The Crom Yews: Summer Evening by Lough Erne

Snow: the Fortingall Yew - with Eagle

WE spent a few days at Pitlochry in the Highlands of Scotland and one of our excursions was the long, lonely drive into the heights of Glen Lyon. Said to be Scotland's longest and most beautiful glen, the narrow road winds its way through the mountains from the shores of Loch Tay and follows the course of the crystal clear River Lyon for most of the way. This long, lonely and at times dramatic route passes very few communities and yet the area is rich in history and lore.

At Fortingall, for example, from where we began this trek, there stands Europe's oldest piece of vegetation. It is a yew tree which is estimated to be more than 3000 years old. The old tree has a chequered history, suffering from the lighting of fires within its ancient trunk to having pieces hacked off for making bows. But it has survived. Today, the tree is surrounded by a wall and a protective fence, but it continues to thrive in this lonely Scottish glen.

The tiny village of Fortingall boasts some delightful thatched cottages; it was also the site of a Roman camp and this has produced one of the most astonishing stories of this region. King Metallanus ruled the Scots from 10BC to 29AD and he lived at

Fortingall. It seems he was a very fair man and his reign was noted for the peace and security it brought. The Roman Emperor, Caesar Augustus, sent an envoy to meet this peaceful Scots ruler; the envoy was accompanied by some soldiers as his escort and the Roman party built a small camp at Fortingall. They lived here for about a year and there is little doubt that King Metallanus introduced the soldiers to some of his family and to the local girls.

One of the Scots lasses gave birth to a son and that boy was taken back to Rome by the soldiers when they departed a year later. His name was Pontius Pilate. The legend that Pontius Pilate was born in this tiny Highland village has never been disproved, but it is one of which local people are not particularly proud. The descendants of King Metallanus are the renowned Menzies family of Scotland and the tradition says that it was a member of the Menzies family (pronounced Mengies) who was the mother of Pontius Pilate. Or should it be Pontius McPilate?

High in this fabulous glen there are two lochs - Loch an Daimh and Loch Lyon, and it was not far from the banks of Loch Lyon that we picnicked as a buzzard soared overhead, mewing like a cat as it searched the ground for its own lunch. We realised that we were among history here, with memories of clan battles and stirring deeds about us as we travelled this lonely road with only a buzzard for company. The place was deserted but the entire glen is rich with folk lore, as indicated through the Black Watch monument, General Wade's bridge, Weem Cowpack, the Stone of the Dead, Iron Well, McNab's Hollow, the Bodach Stone, the Stone of the Sandal, a Celtic fort and former castles full of heroic Scots tales.

NICHOLAS RHEA

Box

Buxus sempervirens. *Semper*, means 'always' and *vivum* means 'alive'. Box is another Time Lord that hangs onto life with great tenacity wherever it grows or is grown. Deutero Isiah (one of the five great seers who together yet in isolation across the ancient world found a spirituality in creation which links all the religions and religious philosophies of the world) knew of box, and so in probability did many, for trade routes in precious things even then spanned much of the civilized world. Its hard, close-grained wood was used to make many things including the best of flutes. The Romans held this most diminutive of the Time Lords growing to a maximum of ten metres, sacred to the wind whose god was Mercury. The Greeks linked the tree to death and used it as a shrine tree as did the British until recent times.

William Wordsworth, said to be one of the fathers of British botany, bemoaned the fact that although it grew wild in plenty on steep mountain sides in Germany 'but in England it groweth not by itself, in any place I know, though there is much in England'.

The Romans may well have planted it wherever they could as local supplies for civic and religious occasions: Box Hill in Surrey could be one such place, for it occurs in great abundance along with yew on those steep chalk slopes. At Boxwell there are almost forty acres of this tree on the steep side of a narrow Cotswold valley. However there is now proof enough that it is a native to these shores and has grown on the chalk of the Arun Gap and other places since it arrived before global warming filled up the English Channel.

In 1695, John Ray was the first botanist to describe its close growing trees that form a dense canopy overhead. The inside of such woods stink of foxes, and John Evelyn, who lived not far from Box Hill, wrote that 'the smell is driving Box out of gardens', although he also suggested that it should be planted for the excellency of its wood. Indeed its dense timber was much prized for making all manner of hard wearing things, not least the rulers of the classroom that whacked mathematics across many schoolchild's knuckles. John Aubrey said that the comb makers of London purchased the wood from Boxley near Maidstone and Box Hill. So valuable was the timber that it was sold by weight not by volume. Wild or planted this tough plant gave the gardeners of Elizabeth I great licence with the 'I would be a Tree' spirit of this Time Lord: by using it to edge small flower beds of intricate shape and pattern. Thus they discovered the art of the *parterre* and developed the craft of topiary.

Candlemas Eve

Down with the rosemary and bays,
Down with the mistletoe;
Instead of holly, now up-raise
The greener box, for show.

The holly hitherto did sway;
Let box now domineer,
Until the dancing Easter-day,
Or Easter's eve appear.

Then youthful box, which now hath grace
Your houses to renew,
Grown old, surrender must his place
Unto the crisped yew.

ROBERT HERRICK

Blizzard on Box Hill

Exotica

EXOTIC in Time Lord parlance means from another place and not a native of these shores, but, as we have seen in Britain, this is set against the oh so short timescale of the end of the last glaciation. The ice sheets had swept these islands clear of all trees and most of its vegetation and, as they melted, the oceans rose to give rise once more to the worldwide stories of the Great Flood.

Providing Britain with its ultimate protection from attack and as a deterrent to colonisation and conquest, the English Channel at its narrowest is just twenty-two miles of salty water.; those plants and animals that made their way back of their own accord are called native while all others that needed the help of modern Noahs to make the crossing should be called exotic. That may be so to a boring academic, but to others the word has connotations of beauty, strangeness, and eroticism, and certainly many Time Lords have been brought here and planted for those and other reasons. Be that as it may, if we push the timescale back we find the word 'native' more difficult to define. Take for example the ginkgo which, since its discovery growing in Temple Gardens in China, has been a 'must have' for those rich enough to have one growing in their demesne. Long before it was discovered living in China, its peculiar maiden hair leaves were known from the fossil record as was the fact that they were an important food for the vegan members of the terrible lizards, including those that left their footprints deep and clear in England's own Jurassic Park. So what's new and what's native in the parlance of the Time Lords? So humbled by our timescale, 'exotic' takes on its more ancient meaning: 'things we have a craving for or anything that tickles our fancy'. So what could be more exotic than palms in Cornwall, hilbilly hickory in Antrim, figs and magnolias in Saint James's Park near Buckingham Palace? Perhaps the only saving grace of our modern tinpot politicians is that they love to be seen planting ceremonial trees, many of which are 'exotics'. Why oh why don't they do something to stop the wanton destruction of the piteous scraps of old growth forest our world still has left?

Artistic licence further clouds the picture for the laburnum is a true native of Britain just as the strawberry tree is a true native of Ireland, the latter just one of many plants that picked out the warm wet, frost free route by which the Celtic people brought their beliefs in the 'spirituality of the golden bough of the Time Lords' to Britain. Legend has it that the mother sacred grove was ruled by a king who had the favours all the wood nymphs had to offer: cool shade, pure water, fruits in due season, the richness of the hunt and lust for the exotic. All was his until the moment of his death when his murderer took on his role and all the pleasures and the one final problem that went with it.

With the invention of printing in 400 AD in China and about a thousand years later in Europe, the annual clatter of mallets on wood blocks carved with characters and letters, and later the ring of the printing press, took over from the Time Lords in recording environmental change. Despite the fact that paper is mainly made of trees, it is usually softwoods that sadly record how both diarist, editor, compositor and publisher can be tainted by the worm of sensational prejudice. Not so this book, for it tells the story as recorded in the annual rings of the Time Lords of Britain punctuated with giga-grains of truth.

Last Hickory at Kenmore House: Londonderry on August Evening

Down ducks are dabbling, up tails all ...

TRADITIONAL NURSERY RHYME

Sunset: Fig Trees, Saint James's Park, London

Nunc viridi membra sub arbuto
Stratus, nunc ad aquae lene caput sacrae.

His limbs outstretched now beneath a green Strawberry tree,
now beside the gentle head of a sacred stream.

HORACE ODES 1, 21 - 22

Horace refers to someone enjoying a picnic at an idyllic country spot under a hybrid strawberry tree native to Mediterranean lands, or possibly the Cyprus or Eastern one so common in Aegean parts; but ours in comparison is usually a large, sturdy and still evergreen bush called *arbutus unedo* and found in south and south-west Europe and south-west Ireland. It belongs to the family *ericaceae* which includes the rhododendron and heath and heather and is included in the genus *arbutus* which includes the North American madrona laurel or madrono *arbutus menziesii*, a tree which can reach 120 feet and yield valuable timber.

Just twelve thousand years ago there was land extending south of Ireland which adjoined Cornwall and Brittany and these trees were one of the few species surviving from the great ice sheet to the north and east. Though not as tall and grand as the hybrid variety - there is a superb one in Kew Gardens - they do particularly well around Killarney's peaty, frostless shores. Curiously, a gardener will tell you that they do well on chalk soils too. It is one of our best autumn through winter flowering trees and, unlike its muddy, scaly bark, is attractive with its small round strawberry-like fruits which, also produced in the autumn, quickly ripen and fall in October. *Unedo*, the Latin name, is supposedly an abbreviation of 'I only eat one' such is its fruit's disgusting taste. While John Evelyn noted in *Silva* that the tree was 'too much neglected by us, the seventeenth-century herbalist, John Pechey, recommended a concoction of the strawberry tree's flowers and fruits as an antidote to plague!

Arthur Young, an eighteenth-century English agricultural journalist wrote in September 1776 after boating on Lough Leane near Killarney in Kerry:

Near to the wood of Glena [exactly similar but to the west from this picture's woods] takes on the appearance of one immense sweep hanging in the most beautiful manner imaginable. It is one deep mass of wood, composed of the richest shades perfectly dipping in the water ... Glena woods having more Oak, and some Arbutus's are the finer and deeper shades.

The highest peaks in Ireland are the Macgillycuddy's Reeks a few miles west from the scene depicted here.

Bather: Strawberry Tree, Killarney

Second Encounter

Down this lovely street of church and walls of gracious stone,
past a plaque telling me I'm at St Mary's in Magdalen Street,
expecting nothing and caring less,
I met a light I had not met before,
and pulled up beside an iron gate.
Before me stood a tree in sun,
whose light poured off its frothy rim.
Rosy fingers of purple pods
waved at me weightless through leaves,
curved and elegant in simplicity.

The light and dainty thing spilled over the sunlit honey wall,
like some charming prisoner in a zoo, soliciting a treat, sympathy,
proud for all its Grace. Cercis Siliquastrum;
from some deep well I spoke its name aloud.
No disgrace, no evil heavy fruit could ever hang
on such a fragile tree, lest both together fall.
I blew a kiss, and light poured over me.

MARGARET WHYTE

Judas Tree: Sunday Morning, Magdalen Road, Bath

THE slope is darkly sprinkled
With ancient Junipers,
Each a small secret tree:
There not a branch stirs.

I fear those waiting shapes
Of wry, blue-berried wood.
They make a twilight in my mind,
As if they drained my blood.

LAURENCE BINYON

The common juniper is one of the three conifers native to Britain

Juniper Bushes: Fairfield from Easedale

Tulip Tree, Cornwall

The Origin of the Curious Shaped Tulip Tree's Leaf

SHAPELY curvaceous leaf
from trembling Tulip tree
was plucked by rampant Adam
in hoist immodesty.

'I don't care a fig for those knickers!'
screamed Eve tearing part away.
The leaves have curtailed, concave bottoms
since foremost bottom's display.

PIERS BROWNE

Magnolia

Exotic stranger, whose most costly scent
Might, with sweet odour, flood a Continent,
Whose opulent voluptuousness looks down
Amazed upon an English country town,
(So Messalina, exiled, might we see
Brooding, astonished, at a Parish tea) -
What do you here, lost Empress? How old
Our sun must seem, our warmest wind, how cold!
What thoughts are yours? Those petals of thick cream
Lie lapped and laved in a continuous dream
Of forests, dark as death, yet shining bright
With tropic blooms, all insolence and might,
Which poison with hot breath the violent air,
Their frantic perfume heavy like despair!

LADY MARGARET SACKVILLE

The magnolia is one of the most noble
of an aristoctratic family with a place in
every garden.

FRED WHITSEY

Magnolia on Magnolia, Lover on Lover:
St James's Park, London

WISTERIA

I swear's gone mauve
quite bordering hysteria.
Such blooms wistfully droop
off dark bough's writhing loop
that the name's stiffly onomatopoeia.

PIERS BROWNE

Herb Garden, Fulham Palace: with Wisteria, Mimosa and Cat

The Ginkgo Tree and the Dagger Moths

Blaze of May
smarag'd viridian
sliding torrent of
greensleaves
Emperor's Tree
of Life and Rising Sun
Ginkgo Biloba
lures the grey daggers
to betray
bright wings
on dark maidenhair

MARGARET WHYTE

Almost as common as the honey locust in New York City is the tree whose memories are the most ancient of all. This is the ginkgo - the Tree Who remembers the dinosaurs. It seems that no animal alive today disperses ginkgo fruit in the wild, and though surely something was dispersing it at least in a haphazard way during most of the last 65 million years, the fruit itself has evolved to attract small, carrion-feeding dinosaurs. Male ginkgoes are preferred as street trees today because rotting ginkgo fruit smells like vomit (hence the theory that only carrion feeders would find it attractive). Nevertheless, some parks and sidewalks in New York are shaded by females that produce prolific fruit. Only because this Jurassic-age tree is virtually indestructible to insects, unappealing to herbivores big and small, and capable (like cottonwood) of sprouting from ancient rootstock again and again, did ginkgo survive for millions of years after its intended seed dispersers had become ghosts. Only because humans in China began to cultivate the tree for medicinal values of its leaves and seeds was ginkgo - once ranging through temperate climates of the Northern Hemisphere - rescued from oblivion.

We humans are now in partnership with ginkgo, as we are with honey locust and countless other trees. Missing their partners in evolution, these trees now depend on us...

CONNIE BARLOW

Ginkgo and Grey Daggers: in Thunderstorm

Acer atropurpureum: *Welsh Borders*

F REQUENTLY with serious works and ones of great import, some purple patch or other is stitched on, to show up far and wide.

HORACE from ARS POETICA

The Handkerchief Plot

An estate of new houses as clean as a pin,
posh and exciting just right to move in;
all stages and sizes with Grandma or dog,
why don't you deposit and go for a jog?

A nice healthy lifestyle, nice neighbours too.
No leylandii needed for nice folks as you.
Lawns, dogs and kids' bikes, the good life is here;
barbeques, blasters, and sixpacks of beer.

Leave mess behind, move out to the site
that's green and not brown, open and light.
All's ready and instant, need no plan or design,
it's intended to save you money and time.

There's even a tree in each front of each house,
grown instantly for you, as cute as a mouse.
Handkerchief tree in a blandkerchief land.
Brick fields forever in Suburbiastan!

MARGARET WHYTE

*The Jones' and Handkerchief Trees,
Somewhere in the South-east*

A PLENTEOUS place is Ireland for
    hospitable cheer,
Uileacan dubh O!
There is honey in the trees where her
    misty vales expand,
Uileacan dubh O!
And her forest paths in summer are
    by falling waters fanned.
There is dew at high noontide there,
    and springs i' the yellow sand,
On the fair hills of Ireland.

SAMUEL FERGUSON *from* THE FAIR HILLS OF IRELAND

THE interaction between trees and the Earth's atmosphere is most commonly associated with their critical update of carbon dioxide. Species such as eucalyptus, however, also have an enormous impact on the chemical reactions occurring within the atmosphere itself. Although rare in Britain, they are widespread throughout the tropics, and every year their leaves release millions of tonnes of the chemical isoprene as part of a natural cycle that has occurred for hundreds of thousands of years. The interaction between tree emissions and man's pollution can lead to the generation of harmful smog and a reduction in visibility. This interaction is often exacerbated by commercial forestry practices that plant non-indigenous species from cooler climates to maximise tree growth rates. Non-indigenous species when transplanted to warmer regions often release increased quantities of their natural emissions, which can in turn interact with local pollution; a dramatic example has been eucalyptus commercial forestry in the Mediterranean, where thick smogs are now often seen over forested areas.

DR ALISTAIR LEWIS

Editor's note: It is hoped that the koala bear which lives off the leaves of eucalypti is alert enough to realise that under extremely high temperatures the tree can self-combust. It is also hoped that, unlike the Portuguese today, we do not plant new eucalyptus forests near villages since wells and springs can quickly dry up. Such is this tree's thirst we too might self-combust in droughts.

Gigantic Eucalyptus: Summer Morning, Garron Tower, County Antrim

The Passionate Shepherd to his Love

COME live with me and be my love,
And we will all the pleasures prove
That valleys, groves, hills and fields,
Woods or steepy mountain yields.

And we will sit upon the rocks,
Seeing the shepherds feed their flocks
By shallow rivers, to whose falls
Melodious birds sing madrigals.

And I will make thee beds of roses,
And a thousand fragrant posies,
A cap of flowers, and a kirtle,
Embroidered all with leaves of myrtle.

A goqn made of the finest wool
Which from our pretty lambs we pull,
Fair lined slippers for the cold
With buckles of the purest gold.

A belt of straw and ivy buds,
With coral clasps and amber studs,
And if these pleasures may thee move,
Come live with me, and be my love.

The shepherds' swains shall dance and sing
For thy delight each May-morning;
If these delights thy mind may move,
Then live with me, and be my love.

CHRISTOPHER MARLOWE

Myrtle: *Awaiting the Second*

Summer Dawn: Palm near Lymington

T HE palm, the palm, on English earth alarm!
Strew the yew at Easter, so you sing out hymn and psalm.

ANON

The word palm is no longer used as a synonym for yew in today's Britain because, until the Reformation, the ends off a yew's distinct and dark green branches were substituted for the then unavailable palm leaves and carried in processions on Palm Sundays, or left in static church decoration all over the Easter period. If one has a head for heights, defoliating from palm trees like this splendid one, might bring back both tradition and authenticity into church.

THEN it was the Muse of Painting came to my rescue - out of charity and out of chivalry, because after all she had nothing to do with me...

Happy are the painters, for they shall not be lonely. Light and colour, peace and hope, will keep them company to the end, or almost to the end of the day.

WINSTON CHURCHILL

Nobel prizewinner in 1953 for literature, Churchill was describing in *Painting as a Pastime*, how the painting bug bit him when he was cast down in misery after the First World War's disastrous Dardanelles campaign.

Laburnum: towards the Weald - Forest Ridges - from Chartwell

Now England's glades unwinter brilliantly,
The sun's a gold-giver in every village,
Daisies galore, small glory of meadows,
All thrill my convictions to voyage.
Also the sorrow-tones of remore cuckoos
Bode badly. That same bluff citizen
Knows next to nothing of anxious solitudes. -
And yet my heart-boat tugs at harbour ropes,
I imagine already the plunging whales,
Sea-distances surge through my dissatisfaction,
Already the gannet screams to itself
Over forlorn water, kingdom of roaming whales,
All, all irresistible to this sea-yearning.

FROM THE SEAFARER

TRANSLATED FROM THE ANGLO-SAXON BY HAROLD MASSINGHAM

Summer Palms: South Cornwall

Woods

WOODS is a word with two linked but different meanings. If the one encapsulates the fantastic range of Mother Nature's own renewable resource that has served people so well and in so many ways since they erupted onto the evolutionary scene, the other relates to the sociology of the Time Lords themselves, the woodlands in which they grow. Like people, plants form relationships with each other and their environment, and along the Atlantic coast of Europe there were five main types of woodland: silver and downy birchwoods that graced the montane regions above the level of pine and oak, their ground layer dominated with grasses or bilberry, and the famous forests of *pinus, sylvestris* var *scotica*, scots pine which grew with downy birch, alder, aspen and rowan mainly on the flanks of the mountains; to the east, south and west of this there once stretched the oak woods in all their glory, the two oaks consorting with grey poplar, aspen, the two birches, alder, wych elm, crab apple, wild cherry, yew and holly, depending on latitude, longitude, aspect and bedrock; beech, along with hazel, field maple, spindle, box and elder, were found on calcareous soils in the south, while wet woodlands of grey willow, hawthorn, spindle, buckthorn, alder buckthorn and privet flanked streams, rivers and wetlands.

What it must have been like to try to travel through this sylvan world of a mere eight thousand years ago we can only guess at, for all our wild woods have been destroyed or altered out of all recognition. The good news is that across the length and breadth of Britain people of every class, colour and creed are beginning to work in partnership to put back the balance of native trees into our landscapes and into our lives in new national forests and sacred groves in which the Time Lords will take down all the evidence.

In my craft or sullen art
Exercised in the still night
When only the moon rages
And the lovers lie abed
With all their griefs in their arms,
I labour by singing light
Not for ambition or bread
Or the strut or trade of charms
On the ivory stages
But for the common wages
Of their most secret heart.

Not for the proud man apart
From the raging moon I write
On these spindrift pages
Nor for the towering dead
With their nightingales and palms
But for the lovers, their arms
Round the griefs of the ages,
Who pay no praise or wages
Nor heed my craft or art.

DYLAN THOMAS

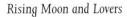

Rising Moon and Lovers

Wooded Shoreham: June Evening

SHOREHAM in Kent has some good mature oak and beech woods, but much much more two hundred years ago when Samuel Palmer arrived from London, where he was born in 1805, to convalesce from illness. He stayed seven years. In his oils and etchings he fostered the idyll of simple rustic life: shepherds and shepherdesses love each other, their flocks, their sunrises, sunsets, full moons and always the frothy, wholesome, burgeoning summer days wherein grew his special curiously oversized grasses and foliage. A well-known picture, *The Bright Cloud*, contains a burgeoning great cumulus cloud as the subject and is alone better known than most of the other pictures he did for nearly fifty years, such as the huge picturesque Neapolitan vistas so beloved of Victorian drawing-rooms.

In Shoreham a small colony of artists met in Palmer's day, artists like John Varley, really a classical painter of the history genre, and John Linnell who met the aged William Blake in 1813 and who became father-in-law to Palmer. The group became known to the locals as 'The Extollagers' because, probably after much cider taking, they would at eventide, quite unprovoked, amiably but loudly extol to all and sundry about the beauties of a rural life.

BREATHES there the man with soul so dead,
Who never to himself hath said,
This is my own, my native land!

WALTER SCOTT *from* LAY OF THE ANCIENT MINSTREL

Once the subject of much legend of Evil Ones and Fairie Queens, of all the fine views in his beloved Borderland, this, 'Scott's View', was Sir Walter's favourite. So much so, that as the horses drew his coffin to his last resting place (which against much opposition he chose as nearby Dryburgh Abbey) they stopped here out of their master's habit to pause for exactly ten minutes to gaze across the great loop of the Tweed's meander towards the Eildon Hills.

Though drawn from a different angle, this piece below sums up the frisson Scott must have felt each time he thus feasted his eyes:

THERE are certain views in all countries which must quicken the heart of the man who sees them after an absence. Such is the sight of Scotland from Carter Bar. It is a tender, lovely view. This is not 'Caledonia stern and wild': it is Scotland in a homely, gracious mood with a smile on her lips, a welcome in her eyes, a cake on the girdle, a kettle on the hob. It is a view of Scotland which burnt itself into the brain of the greatest of all Borderers - Walter Scott. It would be impossible, I think, for any Scotsman returning home by Carter Bar after years of foreign place to hold back a shout or perhaps a tear. It is so authentically Scotland and could be nowhere else. It seemed to me, as I stood there looking down into the valley, that here was something as definite and unmistakable to a Scotsman as the White Cliffs of Dover to an Englishman.

The heathery moors slope down to a distant valley. The sun is setting. The sky above the Lammermuirs is red and troubled. The wind drops. The autumn mists far below are creeping from wood to wood. The smoke from chimneys hangs motionless in the air. Thin veils of grey wrap themselves around the foothills. Faint white serpents of mist twist above the greenwood, outlining the course of stream and river. It is a study in blue. In the foreground, like a promise of the Highlands, and as notable as a ship at sea, rise the tall peaks of the Eildon Hills, blue as hothouse grapes, standing with their feet among the foothills of the Tweed ...

H. V. MORTON *from* IN SEARCH OF SCOTLAND

Meander of the Tweed: towards Melrose

Buzzard in Somerset: from the Quantocks

Now, my friends emerge
Beneath the wide wide Heaven - and view again
The many-steepled tract magnificent
Of hilly fields and meadows, and the sea,
With some fair bark, perhaps, whose sails light up
The slip of smooth clear blue betwixt two isles
Of purple shadow! ...

SAMUEL TAYLOR COLERIDGE: MY PRISON from THIS LIMB-TREE BOWER

Incapacitated due to an accident, Coleridge imagines what his friends would see on their walk on the Quantocks in June 1797 as he sits beneath a lime tree in his cottage garden at Nether Stowey in north Somerset. His frustration can be gauged if one realises that he, like Wordsworth, his greatest friend on these Quantocks walks, was a passionate walker. Indeed when in the Lakes, Coleridge climbed Scafell Pike, at 3210 feet the highest mountain in England, and descended by running down the most difficult side of it! This he did without Wordsworth who was incapacitated, doubt-less, by his Muse or his womenfolk.

What is both hilariously absurd is that during their time in the Quantocks, Coleridge and Wordsworth were tracked and recorded by a Home Office spy set on discovering whether the two eccentric hiker-poets were in league with the dastardly revolutionary French and set on finding a landing-place for invasion!

FORGET six counties overhung with smoke,
Forget the snorting stream and piston stroke,
Forget the spreading of the hideous town;
Think rather of the pack-horse on the down,
And dream of London, small and white and clean,
The clear Thames bordered by its gardens green;
Think, that below bridge, the green lapping waves
Smite some few keels that bear Levantine staves,
Cut from the yew-wood on the burnt-up hill,
And pointed jars that Greek hands toiled to fill,
And treasured scanty spice from some far sea,
Florence gold cloth, and Ypres napery,
And cloth of Bruges, and hogsheads of Guienne;
While nigh the thronged wharf Geofrrey Chaucer's pen
Moves over bills of lading - mid such times
Shall dwell the hollow puppets of my rhymes.

WILLIAM MORRIS from THE EARTHLY PARADISE, PROLOGUE

Spring's Yellow Leafage: all London from 'Ally Pally'

Tree Poem

THE leaves
have all left,
but the tree
will be
all right.

JOHN HEGLEY

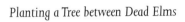

Planting a Tree between Dead Elms

Cone of Douglas Fir

List Of Illustrations

AND some scarce see Nature at all ...

WILLIAM BLAKE

UNTIL he reached the age of nine or ten
He lived in places north of Birmingham,
At first at Beeston, Nottinghamshire, and then
In Eccles, Lancashire, where he began
At school to learn by heart the wizard words
That, he was told, were known as "poitry",
Words that soared and swooped and sang like birds,
Or rumbled in the dark mysteriously.

The vowel in "poitry" rhymed, of course, with "boy".
Next, the family moved south, a place
Not far from London where they might enjoy
A better life - though this proved not the case -
And here at school he heard an alien sound:
The teacher spoke of "poetry", the first
Syllable rhymed with cockney "dough". He found
His mind befogged, but then the mist dispersed.

Suddenly he saw the marvellous thing
Quite plain in silvery sunlight, tall, serene
Against the blue sky, its branches blossoming
In multicoloured vocables from green
Syllabic buds, the flowering Poet Tree,
Where for centuries fabled birds had sung,
And under whose protecting canopy
Poets had dreamed, or from its branches swung.

VERNON SCANNELL

TWO-thirds of the world's original forests have been destroyed, and at this rate over three-quarters will have disappeared within twenty years from this book's publication.

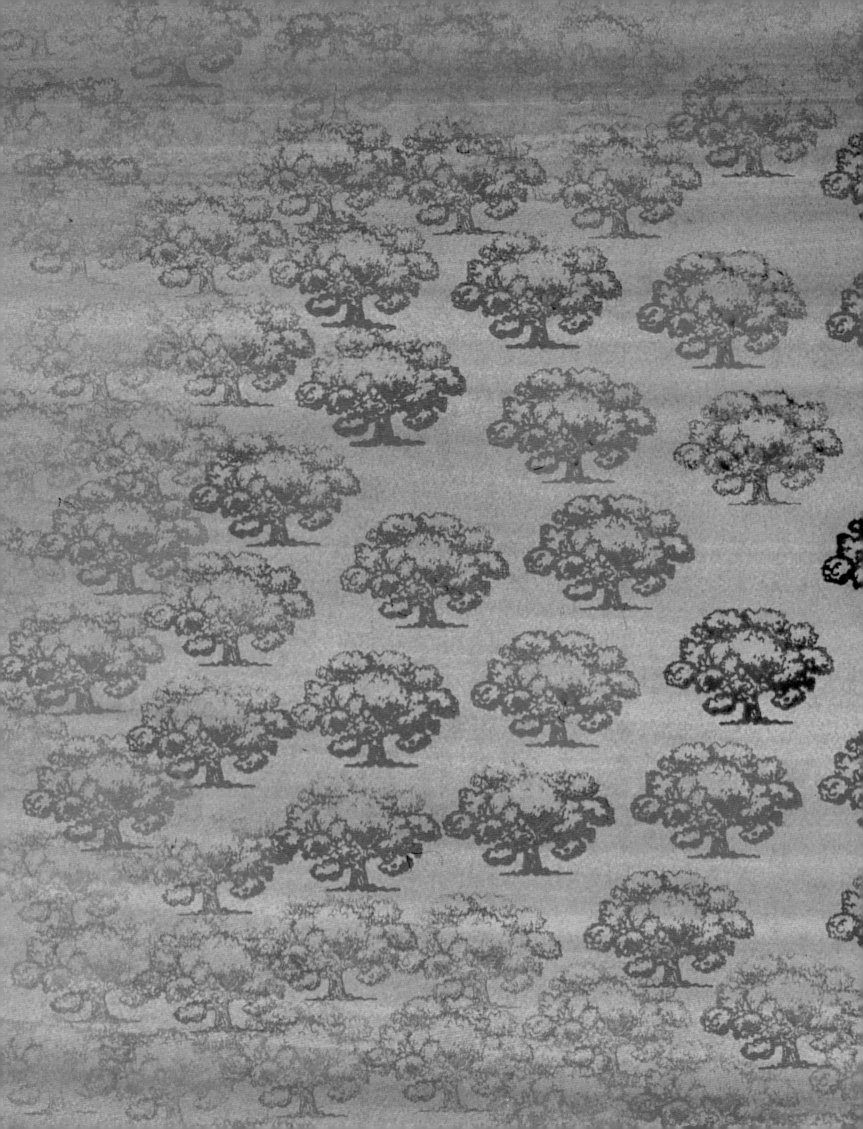